# YOUR
# JAZZ
# COLLECTION

DEREK LANGRIDGE

# YOUR
# *Jazz*
# COLLECTION

ARCHON BOOKS & CLIVE BINGLEY

FIRST PUBLISHED 1970 BY CLIVE BINGLEY LTD
THIS EDITION SIMULTANEOUSLY PUBLISHED IN THE USA
BY ARCHON BOOKS, THE SHOE STRING PRESS INC,
995 SHERMAN AVENUE, HAMDEN, CONNECTICUT 06514
PRINTED IN GREAT BRITAIN
COPYRIGHT © DEREK LANGRIDGE 1970
ALL RIGHTS RESERVED
208 01061 0

# Contents

*page*

CHAPTER 1: THE COLLECTOR

The nature of collecting 9
Book and record collecting 15
Jazz collecting 21
Readings 40

CHAPTER 2: THE COLLECTOR'S AIDS

Institutions 44
Research and discography 48
The principal discographies listed 53
Jazz book collecting 55
Bibliographies, encyclopedias etc 57
The principal reference books listed 59
Categories of jazz writing 61
Selected examples of jazz writing 68
Readings 71

CHAPTER 3: THE COLLECTION—1 CLASSIFYING AND INDEXING
THE LITERATURE

Arrangement and indexing of books 73
A classification for the literature of jazz 80
Sample arrangement of books 105
Sample index of articles 111
Readings 129

CHAPTER 4: THE COLLECTION—2 ARRANGEMENT AND
INDEXING OF RECORDS

Methods of arranging records 130
A classification for jazz records 142
Indexing the records 145
Readings 153

INDEX 155

# *Preface*

Although addressed primarily to the private collector, this book should be equally useful to the librarian. Private collecting and librarianship are, or should be, two manifestations of the same activity. Since the librarian is a professional, and therefore regularly practising acquired skills, it is easier for him to make use of a book written for amateurs than for amateurs to make use of one written for professionals.

On the subjects of classification and indexing I write as a professional, but I have endeavoured to make my explanations intelligible to anyone without previous experience or familiarity with the jargon. On the subject of jazz I write as a collecting amateur and not as a professional critic. Since personal taste and selection are of the essence in collecting, I make no apology for the fact that my *examples* are drawn mainly from traditional and mainstream jazz. This in no way affects the general validity of the *principles* I have discussed.

To avoid overloading the text, full citations for books and articles discussed have been collected in the reading lists.

For assistance in various ways my thanks are due to Richard Allen, Dave Carey, Charles Fox and Richard Spottswood.

DEREK LANGRIDGE

November 1969

# *The collector*

THE PHENOMENON OF COLLECTING: Although there are plenty of books and articles on specific forms of collecting there is comparatively little writing which discusses the subject in general. I know of only one comprehensive study, *Lock, stock and barrel: the story of collecting*, by Douglas & Elizabeth Rigby. It was published in the United States in 1944 and has long been out of print. This is a pity, because apart from being unique (as far as I am able to ascertain) it is also as good a survey as one could imagine. Nearly half of its 500 pages are devoted to a history of collecting, from the earliest civilizations up to modern America. Here we scale the olympic heights of collecting and observe the activities of emperors, kings, princes and wealthy businessmen. The emphasis is on art treasures, rare books, and objects of scientific interest. The remainder of the book has equal relevance to the humbler forms. It is a thorough and well-balanced study of the motives, methods and amenities of collecting.

It is particularly surprising that psychologists have not paid more attention to the subject: there is very little to be found in *Psychological abstracts*, a publication that goes back as far as 1927. Earlier writers, such as William James and William McDougall, regarded collecting as a manifestation of the acquisitive instinct, and saw miserliness and kleptomania as morbid exaggerations of the same impulse. The only evidence they adduce is that most children collect something at some time. Sir Kenneth Clark, in an article on ' The great private collections ', also refers to collecting as an instinct. ' The collector's instinct, if animals and children are any guide, has two roots; the desire to pick up anything bright and shining and the desire to complete a series . . .' The only animal I can see here is a red herring. Many objects of collecting are anything but bright and shining, and

9

I would like to know what animal has the power of forming the concept of completing a series. Such accounts completely fail to explain why only some people continue to be collectors in later life. It seems to me that Katherine Whitehorn, in an article called 'Magpies' (*Spectator*, October 5 1962), was much nearer the truth. She first distinguishes between 'pure collecting' and several things which look like it but are not: having several of something you really like; the 'magpie instinct', which makes some people want to acquire everything they see; and the 'squirrel instinct'—never throwing anything away. Later in the essay she gives a positive definition. 'There is an urge . . . to get one fragment of life, however small, absolutely under control. It may be only match-box lids of the year 1900, but their collector not only knows all about them, he actually possesses one of each: he has them taped. It is the desire to fill in completely one small area . . .'

If there are no 'pure' collectors, without some element of acquisitiveness or one-up-manship, it is still possible to distinguish between pathological and normal collecting. The Rigbys make the point well in their book: 'Many of the "collecting manias" or "peculiar" hobbies, as distinguished from more normal collecting pursuits, are explainable as growing out of specific compulsions or repressions . . . it is by and large true that collecting manias—less closely related to true collecting than they appear—may vanish should the repressions causing them be lifted, whereas the true collector's love for his items and his field usually remains unshaken to the grave.'

My earlier objection to Sir Kenneth Clark's description referred to the suggestion that collecting was an instinct. Instinctive behaviour is what we have in common with animals; this activity is peculiarly human. It is an aspect of the search for wholeness, for perfection. Not only does the collector want a complete series, he also wants each item as far as possible in its perfect, original condition. My own view, therefore, is that collecting is an activity which has symbolic value, irrespective of the intrinsic worth of the objects collected. I doubt whether arguments would convince anyone who doesn't give immediate assent to this proposition, but one point about record collecting is perhaps worth making. Collectors find an attraction in discs that they do not find in tapes. Why? The physical form of books is an important part of the appreciation of their contents, but this is not true of records. Books vary considerably in appearance, but one record is hardly distinguishable from another. Admittedly there are many different labels, but they can hardly be compared with the endless variety of books. The only significant factor that I can discover is shape. Despite their normal method of storage, tapes lack any form. Records are circular, and the circle is a universal symbol of wholeness.

THE VALUES OF COLLECTING

The fundamental element in collecting is a matter of dispute because there is no general agreement on the nature of the human psyche. The values of particular forms of collecting are easier to establish. Two people can agree, for example, on the importance of books while holding entirely different philosophies of life. I suppose that the majority, if asked, would arrange the objects of collecting in a hierarchy, with paintings at the top and beer-mats or match-box labels at the bottom. Art collecting, at least in its higher reaches, differs from other forms in that it is concerned with unique objects. The ordinary laws of supply and demand establish monetary values that put them beyond the reach of all but the very few. This, of course, introduces a number of elements into art collecting which are either absent from other forms or play a very minor part. For this reason the analyses of collectors to be found in art books are not necessarily valid as generalizations. One could hardly ascribe the need for social standing, for example, to the match box collector or even to the record collector.

Monetary values are not intrinsic values. Other, equally valuable products of the human mind are not restricted by the nature of their media as are the visual arts. Even so, they still take a physical form which can perish with time. This means that one of the most important functions in any society is the preservation of its past achievements. From the earliest civilizations this function has been the responsibility of libraries, archives, museums and art galleries. They are an essential complement to educational organizations in the passing on of culture from generation to generation. But no institution is perfect. Much would have been lost but for the contributions of individuals. It has been finely said by John Carter, in *Taste and technique in book collecting*, that ' the book-collector is . . . one of the assault troops in literature's and history's battle against the inequity of oblivion,' that ' collectors . . . have been preservers of books and essential contributors to the progress of scholarship '.

The actions of a society are only the result of individual desires. At present, our western society is losing its feeling for conservation of the past. The America that gave us our jazz music also gave us the philosophy of ' planned obsolescence '. The effect of this may appear to be limited to the manufacture of certain goods, but it is surely merely a symptom of an attitude with far-reaching implications. In an article called ' The sense of the past ', written in 1931, R W Chapman said this: ' We have since learned to distrust the march of mind, and have re-covered the sense of history, the dependence of human affairs upon tradition. If we " are all collectors today ", is not that because we are aware that the Sense of the Past, though it is of the spirit, cannot live without material food?' The desire to conserve the past, which is to be found in the amateur archeolo-gists, the owners of vintage cars and the quixotic protesters against the destruction of the Euston arch, is also an element in the make-up of collectors. The prevalence of collecting in a society is one guarantee of its preservation.

This social value of collecting is strongly emphasised by the Rigbys, and the following quotations summarise their treatment of this theme. 'As the function of collecting is observed to broaden impressively, its history and present and future status begin to assume the proportions of an heroic community monument, for it should not be forgotten that regardless of original motive, the collector has done much to make the history of civilizations and cultures available to us by his persistent preservation of the world's records, physical relics and minutiae. Science is not organized to carry out this huge job in all its details; the time, interest and perseverance to trace the last question on some obscure subject to its lair belong to a thousand thousand collec-tors. By virtue of his curious passion, the collector sees the fascina-tion that lurks in the merest trivia, embraces the small along with the great, and leaves it to posterity to choose between them.

' This record of honourable service is one of the brightest gifts collecting brings to man. From the record, collectors could fashion a telling answer to those detractors who flatly accuse them of crimes of selfishness. Many amateurs are well aware of their mission of preservation, and the following words of two English bibliophiles—one working in the " darkness " of medieval times, the other echoing the same faith in the nineteenth century —are posted as testimony in the name of all good collectors: " We are not only rendering service to God in preparing volumes of new books," wrote Richard de Bury in 1473, " but also exercising an office of sacred piety when we treat books carefully, and again when we restore them to their proper places and commend them to inviolable custody ".

' " It is a good thing to read books, and it need not be a bad thing to write them," declared Frederick Locker-Lampson some four centuries later, " but it is a pious thing to preserve those that have been some time written ".'

' The story of the birth and development of museums and libraries and the collector's vital contribution in this field unfolds in a continuous line from the dawn of civilization into the depths of the future. In Europe there is hardly a great public library or museum which was not originally the private collection of king or nobleman, or which did not draw heavily in its earliest days upon the surviving collections of priests, statesmen and bankers, scientists, antiquarians and citizen amateurs. The collector's work as " guardian of past and present " is on view in every museum in the world. Even in America, which has had no cumulative history of royal collections to build upon, the number of museums and libraries owing their genesis to a robust army of collectors is appreciable, while every institution of the sort in the land is constantly fed from the same source.'

Despite the great importance of this social contribution, my 'defence of collecting' would ultimately rest on the personal satisfaction it gives. The Rigbys describe them as follows: ' From the robot collector to the gifted connoisseur is a long step; as long, let us say in rough comparison, as that between the brick-layer and the architect. The true collector is a person of developed potentials, who uses his native talent through his perception, intuition, integrity, and an abiding love. The more pedestrian collector finds sufficient satisfaction in merely obeying his urge to accumulate. Another relishes most the process of classifying his items, or finds his greatest triumph in completing a series. Within its limits this makes a good game—long, zestful,

13

and reasonably objective—and it is precisely this quality of objectivity that proves to be one of the great amenities. Because of it, collecting can be counted upon as a therapeutic agent, offering release from the demands of the inner self, demands of worry, attention to troublous or monotonous details of life and the distress of loneliness.

'While some devote their best energies to collecting, finding in it the greatest satisfaction life has to offer, other men, busy, successful in business or the professions, discover in collecting a soothing diversion, an interesting relaxation from their careers. Here is a new world with a different set of values, another language, a relief after the day's work. Beyond such diversion and refreshment many ask little more of collecting. For them it is possible to neglect the collection without suffering the pangs of a deprived lover.

'For some, collecting approaches the impersonal systematic preserve of science where one may gratefully forget the emotional plight of man in the contemporary picture, or lose sight of conditions too familiar, too saturated with the personalities of one's environment. Used thus, a collection may be more than mere relaxation. It may be an escape, but the sort of escape which permits one to return to the horsepower world strengthened and heartened.'

For the final word on the subject I turn to *The art of happiness* by John Cowper Powys: ' What everyone needs is some irresponsible undertaking that is at once capable of infinite development and has nothing to do with our regular life's-work or with public success in the world. Some substitute for what we English call a " Hobby " is what *all* human beings require. An " Untouchable " in Calcutta, a beggar in Benares, a gypsy in New York, a composer of fiction for the mob in London, a retired gentleman in Dorset, an emancipated Hareem-Queen in Istanbul, we all, if we are to enjoy any *continuity of happiness,* must hit upon some queer personal enterprise, if it be only watching dung-beetles, or learning Latin, or collecting fossils, or playing the Jews' Harp, or making patchwork quilts, or cutting walking sticks, or studying botany, or adding to our ancestral songs and legends, the mere thought of which, when we wake in the morning, gives us that peculiar glow which only a love-affair or a person's private secret play-passion is able to evoke.'

Of those forms of collecting concerned with objects of intrinsic worth, none is more highly regarded than book collecting. Numerous scholars have written on the subject, and the fascination of books has been exhaustively analysed by Holbrook Jackson in *The anatomy of bibliomania*. In view of their wide scope and long history, this is not surprising. Records cannot compete in either particular, but comparison is justified in their function as a medium for more than one of the great arts. If music was the first beneficiary of records, history and literature were not far behind. The preservation of dramatic performances and authors reading their own work is particularly valuable. Just how valuable may be judged by imagining our reaction now to a contemporary performance of *Hamlet,* or the voice of Chaucer reading the *Canterbury tales.* The musical equivalents are performances by composers and the great interpreters. For those alone the collecting of records is justified, whatever the general value of recordings in relation to live music. The pros and cons have recently been discussed by Yehudi Menuhin and Hans Keller (*Audio and record review,* March and April 1966). Their points were concerned with the nature of recorded performances, but the psychology of listening conditions must also be taken into account. Many people will agree with Colin Wilson who says, in his stimulating book on music called *The brandy of the damned,* that for him the sitting room is the place to listen to music, and that he prefers the gramophone to live music. In the first issue of *The Penguin music magazine* (December 1946), Alec Robertson referred to the advantages of the gramophone and expressed the opinion ' that the regular purchaser of gramophone records, whatever kind of music he may be interested in, is, in general, the most intelligent and best-informed of all music lovers, and certainly the keenest '.

With jazz there can be no argument: the record is its only form of preservation. This means that there are two responsibilities. As much as possible of the music must be recorded, and the products must be kept for posterity. The first function, as with books, is largely left to private enterprise in our society. This works well enough where the demands of profit can be satisfied, but profit does not necessarily coincide with real values. Minority interests in the book world are frequently catered for by institutions, and classical music has been subsidized by national organizations. There is no permanent loss of classical music as long as manuscripts are preserved, but jazz must be caught at the time of its creation. The commercial record companies have caught a considerable amount, but the selection has depended too much on fashion. Since the advent of modern jazz, for example, there has been far too little attention given to the mainstream musicians who created a new style in the thirties, and throughout its history the big companies have steadfastly ignored the music of New Orleans. Once again the importance of collectors has been demonstrated: what we have of this unique and fascinating music is almost entirely due to them. To give just one other example, the only extant recordings of Billie Holiday with the superb backing of the Count Basie band were made by collector John Hammond from a radio broadcast.

In western countries, the preservation of books is well organized. The British Museum, for example, receives by law a copy of everything published in Great Britain. Unfortunately the newer media of communication have not received the same treatment. Neither films nor records are protected in this way by the law. The British Institute of Recorded Sound was not established until 1948 and has never had enough money to buy everything it needs. Gifts of jazz records would always be welcome. There is, of course, a serious problem in the preservation of records which does not arise with books: individual copies have a comparatively short life. New ones can be made only from original masters or from well preserved copies. Existing record companies have not preserved all their masters. Much of the early jazz recording was carried out by small companies who enjoyed a tremendous boom during the twenties and disappeared with the slump. Their story is told by Michael Wyler in *A glimpse at the past* (Jazz Publications, 1957). One of the most important was the Gennet Company whose sad end in 1929 was described by John Davis and G F Gray Clarke in *Jazz forum*, Autumn 1947. A friend of theirs arrived in Richmond to find the plant closed and its material assets for sale. He searched anxiously for matrices, only to find that he was too late to prevent their destruction. In the circumstances it is indeed fortunate that collectors were early enough in the field to save copies of most of these early issues. Many remain collectors' items, available only to the lucky few, but as long as they are in such hands the possibility of reproduction exists. Some of the classic performances now reissued on LP have come in this way from private collections.

Collectors have also played an important part in working for major record companies. John Hammond and Franklin Driggs at Columbia are two of the best known. Others have started their own companies to record neglected musicians or to reissue older recordings. Examples are William Russell's American Music, Gene Williams' Jazz Information, Stephen Smith's HRS, Richard Allen and Orin Blackstone's New Orleans, and Richard Spotts-wood's Melodeon.

## FIRST EDITIONS

Owing to the enormous range of books, there can be more than one kind of collector; but for literature, at least, the essence is in the first edition. There are several reasons for this. First of all, there is the authenticity of the text. The first edition represents the author's original creation in the form approved by him for publication. Subsequent editions may be changed deliberately or by error. This is a matter of scholarship. Secondly, there is the physical form of the book and its appeal to the senses. However ' timeless ' a book may be, it is still a product of a particular time. Its spirit will be only fully expressed in a body born of the same time. This is particularly true of poetry, as Edward Lucie Smith has pointed out in the introduction to a recent catalogue of poetry: ' In a poem, we meet the most physical embodiment of language. The technical devices used by the poet remind us of the whole mechanism of speech. The poet deals in sounds, and he deals in images. These images, in turn, are meant to provoke a physical response in the reader . . . It is an easy step from this to taking an interest in the way that the poem is embodied on the page. To read, for instance, Pound's " Cathay " in the frail little booklet where the poems were originally presented, is, somehow, to get an entirely new insight into what the poet was about.' The last reason is R W Chapman's sense of the past. In the article already quoted he says, ' Even if modern editions were adequate in the information they furnish—and notoriously they are not—they do not satisfy that Sense of the Past without which the study of literature and history is unimaginative and formal '.

Turning to music, we find a similar view in Colin Wilson's

book: ' I find something extraordinarily satisfying,' he says, ' in listening to a recording of a Tchaikowsky aria made in St Petersburg in the 1890's . . .'. But does that satisfaction depend on the copy of the record having been *manufactured* in St Petersburg in the 1890's? Quite clearly it does not. While the music is playing you are not conscious of the record. You *are* conscious of a book the whole of the time you are reading it. I don't deny that there is an antiquarian interest in records, but it is completely divorced from the music and can be satisfied without ever playing them. The appeal of records to the senses and the imagination is obviously not of the essence. We are left with authenticity of text. Does this provide any justification for first edition record collecting?

The text of a record is not as easily modified by accident or design as that of a book. There are, however, a few hazards. Parts of a performance can be left out. A notorious example was the reissue on Emarcy and Fontana of the 1944 Cozy Cole session, which omits the trumpet solos by Joe Thomas (particularly infuriating to admirers of this sadly neglected musician).* Sometimes additions have been made, such as drums to a Jim Hall Trio recording and full orchestration to some Wes Montgomery solos. Fortunately, these practices are rare. More common are the deliberate alteration of sound quality by attempts to simulate stereo recording and the unintentional production of echo by compressing too many tracks on one LP.

Despite the existence of these possibilities, the only major problem is the loss of sound quality merely through the process of transfer. Many collectors of original 78s are convinced that their sound is always superior to that of reissues, and that this does justify first edition collecting. No doubt many reissues are inferior, but this does not prove that they always need be. Transfers can be made without loss and even with improvement. In support of this contention I quote two recent comments on the RCA Vintage Series. Eugene Kramer, in *Coda* June/July 1966 says: 'Another belief that I used to hold may have to be revised if RCA continues the high level of sound reproduction found in the Vintage Series. This belief was that a clean original 78rpm recording always sounds better than a long-play reissue. Now,

* Recently corrected by Mercury on SMWL 21034.

I'm not so sure! The Vintage Series is giving the public the best sounding reissues of jazz recordings perhaps ever produced in North America. Some of the tracks sound even better than mint 78rpm originals! (I feel like a traitor writing this, for I am basically a 78rpm collector who has to justify paying the top dollar for rare originals.)'

The second quotation comes from an article called ' The great music revival ' by John S Wilson, in RCA's magazine *Electronic age,* Summer 1967: 'An unusual aspect of the Vintage Series is that today's listeners actually hear more on the reissue disks than they could when they were originally released:

' " Sound has become as important on Vintage releases as it is in the making of new recordings," says Mike Lipskin who took over the Vintage Series from McCuen in 1965. " People buy Vintage reissues even if they have the original 78rpm shellacs because they have found that the Vintage will be better than the original."

' How can this be?

' The difference is in present day equipment, both the home playback equipment and the studio mastering equipment. When these records were originally released, they were played on wind up machines using soft steel needles that took their form from the shape of the opening grooves (that is why the first few grooves of an old 78 often sound scratchy—these were the grooves that shaped the steel needles). Today's playback cartridges are vastly superior, and their quality is augmented by the equipment available to today's recording engineers.

' The high and low ends of the spectrum, which were compressed or reduced in the original reproduction, can now be brought out to whatever extent they exist on the master recording.'

If such high quality reissues are still the exception rather than the rule, there are many others only slightly inferior to the originals. Some collectors will feel that this loss is amply compensated by elimination of surface noise. Finally, we must recognise that all original records will deteriorate more rapidly and more seriously than books. I conclude, therefore, that as sound quality is the only essential criterion, first editions of records do not hold the same position as first editions of books. There still remains a very important reason for collecting first editions, both in classical music and in jazz. The reason, of course, is that many records have never been reissued. If the masters have been destroyed it is important that copies should be preserved. They may still eventually perish without being reproduced, but while there is life there is hope.

Existence of the masters is no guarantee that records will be reissued and this raises the question of ' pirate ' companies. These arose after the last war when existing copies of jazz records were not sufficient to meet the demands of the greatly increased number of collectors. Many important performances were reissued before the best known ' pirate ' was defeated in court. The American jazz magazine, *The record changer,* always supported the ' pirates ' on the grounds that no private firm had a right to withhold music that belonged to the world. The most amusing incident in the dispute occurred when it was discovered that RCA Victor was actually pressing illegal issues for a ' pirate '. The November 1951 copy of *The record changer* carried in large print on its cover the revelation ' Victor presses Bootlegs '! The editorial made the most of it under the heading 'Art and the dollar '. Without condoning the infringement of rights in general, I agree with *The record changer* in this case. Jazz recordings are unique and unrepeatable performances. If companies that own them will not reissue them or give someone else the right, subsequent infringement of their rights may be illegal but it is not immoral. I believe that the ' pirates ' did influence the major record companies, some of whom have since developed good reissue programmes.

Whether one collects first editions in jazz, then, is a matter of choice. It may arise from a ' pure ' interest in the earlier music or it may include antiquarian and rarity elements. But one doesn't have to concentrate on first editions to be a real jazz collector. There is a near equivalent of the early jazz first edition collector in the collector of old operatic recordings. In his introduction to *The Golden Age recorded,* P G Hurst explains that the book is ' concerned with those who, while possessing a keen musical sense, and a desire to preserve and to understand the highest traditions of the vocal art, have also the collector's urge to seek out objects of curiosity, history, and rarity, and to classify them in a proper manner '. He later distinguishes between antiquarian and non-antiquarian collectors according to whether rarity or intrinsic quality is their chief interest in historical records. ' This happy duality,' he says, ' gives collectors a choice or a combination which they are free to follow, and neither group need exercise themselves unduly over the activities, aims and objects of the other '.

The case for original label jazz collecting has been made by Bill Grauer (*The record changer*, May 1950) and Walter Allen (*Jazz journal*, October 1956). Both have failed to see that the comparison with books is not valid.

## JAZZ FANS AND JAZZ COLLECTORS

It is possible to be interested in jazz and to buy records without being a collector. The jazz public is well analyzed in the most comprehensive study of the music yet published—*The jazz scene* by Francis Newton. After pointing out that the jazz public is overwhelmingly young and masculine, he adds that in later life the interest either disappears entirely or at least loses its intensity. ' Jazz, for the older amateur,' he says, ' is like the occasional dose of lyric poetry for the man who has long ceased to read poetry systematically, a nucleus of surviving youth.' The analogy is a good one: the chief characteristic of both lyric poetry and jazz music is their intensity of expression. The popular association of this with youth is, no doubt, a matter of observed fact, but the belief in its inevitable decline in later life is a false deduction. It is not their youth that people lose, but their life. ' Surviving youth ' is a disparaging expression, which suggests a clinging to the past. It happens, of course, frequently; but it has nothing to do with a continued interest in lyric poetry or jazz. If Robert Graves in his sixties can write some of the finest lyric poems in the English language, if the ' old men ' of New Orleans can create some of the most joyful and exciting performances in jazz, will anyone believe that their audience should be limited to those under twenty five? Francis Newton has referred to the possible awakening of a dormant interest in the middle-aged by a flare of jazz enthusiasm among the young. What he hasn't mentioned is the fact that some people experience their *first* enthusiasm at this time. The explanation of this is simple. There are two crucial periods in life, one at the beginning of youth, the other at the end. Life begins at forty (or thereabouts) on a new uphill path, or it goes steadily downhill on the old one. Adolescence or the beginning of middle-age are the most likely periods for the discovery of creative forces. An excellent case history of the lasting power of jazz and the important part it can play in a person's life is to be found in the autobiography of Burnett James, *Living forwards*.

A love of classical music can be satisfied by mixing ' live ' and gramophone listening in any proportion. ' Live ' listening to jazz has drastic limitations. In time it cuts off the past, in space it reduces to the accident of where one lives. An Englishman who had heard every performance by visiting American musicians would still have heard very little. The real jazz lover must be a record collector. He will be distinguishable from the passing jazz fan not so much by the size of his collection as by the discriminaton and system used in acquiring it.

System is an important characteristic of the true collector, and once again I cannot do better than quote the Rigbys on this point: ' "A collection," according to Webster, " usually implies some order, arrangement, or unity of effort "; and, in the strictest sense of the word, nothing is really a collection which does not partake of these elements. Hence the importance of classification to a good collection. The impulse to classify is primarily the evidence of an active intelligence, since classification is, after all, nothing more nor less than a tool for creating order, a means for arriving at valid interpretation.

' Similarly, that striving for an order and unity which we sometimes call " form " manifests itself in the tendency of the modern collector to specialize, first in one general subject, then progressively in smaller and smaller divisions of that subject, so that by limiting his scope he may, in one field at least, approach the ideal of order and completion ...

' The striving for form also manifests itself in the tendency of modern collectors to follow a specific sequence in forming and arranging collections, as well as in the desire to complete definite " sets " or series of exhibits. The nature of these sequences will vary according to the subject of the collection itself. They may be historical or geographical; they may have to do with size, or with material, or with any of the special classifications evolved by collectors; and in this connection an entire array of rules and regulations develops in each collecting field ...'

SPECIALIZATION IN JAZZ COLLECTING

A complete collection of all jazz records was a feasible objective for the very early collectors. It remains a possibility only to an institution devoted solely to the purpose. The private collector cannot hope to acquire more than a small fraction of what is available. Like book collectors, or collectors of classical recordings, he must specialize. This is not incompatible with maintaining a general interest in the music. In the early days most collectors (except those in some parts of the United States) had to rely solely on their own records and those of friends. Throughout the world today, private collections may be supplemented by live performances, radio and television broadcasts, libraries and jazz clubs.

The limits of a collection may be set in a number of ways. For the convenience of discussion I shall treat these methods as mutually exclusive, although in practice most collections are likely to combine two or more.

### VINTAGE COLLECTING

The most fundamental distinction is between vintage collectors and the rest. Vintage collecting is not a precise category, because the antiquarian interest manifests itself in two ways. In the first place it consists of a preference for earliest forms of the music, and in the second place it includes an interest in old records as physical objects and particularly in first editions. The second criterion would sooner or later allow the inclusion of *any* first edition, but the term vintage collector is normally reserved for 78rpm collectors. The introduction of LP's occurred only shortly after the major development from the earliest forms of the music. The 78rpm record therefore acts as the unifying factor and may be taken as the essence of vintage collecting.

I suppose that the first edition specialists regard themselves as the only true vintage collectors, but I have already given my reasons for not agreeing with this view. It is not my intention to disparage or discourage these specialists. I hope they will continue to perform the valuable function of preserving these rarities and, perhaps even now, occasionally discovering a hitherto unknown item. But at this late date, mere preservation is not enough. The most important service to be performed is the transfer of these rarities to a more durable medium before it is too late.

The coincidence of musical and technical development is no accident. The second world war marks the boundary between two periods in western society in which the whole feeling of life is very different. The 78rpm record belongs to a period much closer in spirit to the Victorian than to our own. It looks like an artefact from a much earlier period, not only for technical reasons, but also for commercial ones. The 78 in its anonymous cardboard cover had to sell on its merits. The LP with its glossy packaging, attractive cover designs and sleeve notes, is a typical product of the present age. Much of this modern presentation is very fine, but commercialism is not entirely beneficial. Its effect on contemporary popular music (including jazz) is discussed in detail by David Dachs in *Anything goes: the world of popular music* (Bobbs-Merrill, 1964).

It is worth pointing out here that a dislike of modern jazz, or a distinct preference for earlier forms, is not necessarily an indication of musical ignorance or naivety. The *essential* difference between styles of music (or of any art) is never technical. Technique is only a means to an end, and if one doesn't like the end the fact that it employs a more advanced or more complex technique is irrelevant. Artists themselves are the most prone to confusing these two things, simply because they are (quite rightly) preoccupied with their own technical problems. In *Jazz: its evolution and essence*, André Hodeir expresses the opinion that ' There are sound reasons for preferring a great modern work to a great classical one '. He takes as examples ' Le sacre du printemps ' and Beethoven's ninth symphony and asks the question. ' Isn't it true that those who prefer the Beethoven work confess implicitly their inability to understand Stravinsky's masterpiece?' I assume from the rest of M Hodeir's writing that he was using ' prefer ' to imply a critical judgment rather than mere taste. Does the ' preference ' by all competent judges for Shakespeare's plays also indicate an inability to understand all later works? The argument is too silly to be worth discussion. The idea of progress is irrelevant to the world of values. Modern jazz is not better than traditional jazz just because it is later. It may produce more outstanding performers, and on the other hand it may produce fewer. It is only the critic, when he is acting as a critic, who needs to be objective about such judgments. As a private person enjoying the music he may have the same kind of preferences as others. Only the auctioneer, said Oscar Wilde, need appreciate all styles of art. Breadth of taste is a relative idea. No one can possibly pursue an interest in all the styles and periods of all the arts of the world.

If a person were only interested in jazz and not in any other kind of music or in any other art, then one could reasonably call his taste limited if he only liked early jazz, or modern jazz. One couldn't say the same of a person with the same preference in jazz but in addition an interest in, say, the whole range of European classical music, some forms of folk music, European literature and painting and some aspects of oriental art.

The collector, as a collector, is the opposite of the objective critic. He is expressing his own personality. It has been said of art collecting that ' Every collection is the public confession . . . of a man who is not, and cannot be, like his fellows '. This is particularly appropriate to a jazz collection, since emphasis on the individual is a major appeal of the music itself. In the present desert of J B Priestley's 'Admass ' jazz is one oasis.

Apart from the psychological factors which mark off the vintage collector, there is also an economic factor which makes vintage collecting the least likely form of specialization to combine with other forms. First editions are very expensive and even reissue 78s often cost considerably more than their equivalent space on an LP. The vintage collector needs all his money for his specialization. Even so, there will be many with antiquarian leanings who cannot afford first editions, and this, together with the sheer scarcity of many items, will lead to the frequent acceptance of 78 reissues as the next best thing. The main disadvantage of these is that gramophone companies were notorious for changing original couplings. The greatest annoyance to English collectors of the 'thirties and 'forties was the forcible yoking together of performances which varied considerably in style, quality or, less serious but equally subversive of system, date of recording. Presumably an element in these changes was the attempt to sell more records, but examination of subsequent LP reissues of early recordings suggests that those responsible just lack the collector's feeling for system. The LP provided a fine opportunity for the issue of complete sets in chronological order, and yet we had to wait over ten years in England for the first issue of this kind (' Louis Armstrong, 1925-1929 ' on Parlophone). Smaller companies, such as the Australian Swaggie and the English VJM, have since been more helpful to collectors in this respect.

There are so many LP reissues available today that the collector can go a long way before he needs to worry about 78s. However, any specialization which includes the early period is likely to need 78s for completion. Not only have many records never been reissued in any form, but some reissues use a different ' take ' from that used on the first occasion. These variant forms of the same tune recorded at one session are invaluable for the light they throw on the nature of jazz improvisation. Any collector of the work of a particular musician will want these variants as much as he wants completely distinct performances.

Some LP reissues include more than one take of a theme. For example, ' The Bix Beiderbecke legend ' (Am RCA, LPM 2323) includes takes 1 and 3 of Whiteman's ' Lonely melody ' and an excerpt from take 1 as well as the whole of take 2 of ' Changes '. A Swaggie reissue of the Rhythmakers includes a rare take of ' Yellow dog blues ' as well as the well known one.

There are also a few large scale issues for which Charles Fox has suggested the name ' variorum ' editions. The Storyville set of the Mezzrow-Bechet King Jazz recordings is one example. Another is the Charlie Parker Savoy series. Limited editions including incomplete takes, false starts and second takes of recording sessions by Tony Parenti, Wild Bill Davison and the Kid Thomas-George Lewis Ragtime Stompers were issued on Jazzology JCE-1, -2 and -3 respectively. These are the jazz equivalents of recordings by Bruno Walter and other conductors in rehearsal. Another little known example of a jazz band rehearsing is a group led by Mary Lou Williams on Folkways FJ2292.

There are at least five current magazines which have a special appeal for the vintage collector: the American *Record research* and *Jazz report,* and the English *VJM, RSVP* and *Storyville.* All five regularly include lists of records for sale. All five have a distinctly archaic appearance, so that their resemblance is much more to the earliest jazz magazines than to their other contemporaries.

THE ANCIENT HISTORY OF JAZZ COLLECTING

78rpm collecting today is the esoteric jazz cult. In the 'twenties and 'thirties *any* interest in jazz was esoteric. The 'forties were the only time when 78rpm collectors were divided into antiquarians on the one hand and those who bought mainly new issues on the other. The element of rarity unites the early collectors and the modern vintage specialists, but the reasons for the rarity have changed. 78s are scarce today partly because they are obsolete, partly because there have been losses in the process of time, and partly because there are more people looking for them. They were scarce in the early days because comparatively few performances had been recorded and very few had been reissued. But scarcity and economic value were not coincident in those days. Before the 'discovery' of jazz, secondhand records could be bought for a few cents in America or a few pence in England. As the number of collectors was quite small, junk shopping was a characteristic mode of acquisition. It is still possible in some American towns, but the subsequent activities of collectors and spread of knowledge have largely eliminated the bargain element in 78rpm collecting in Europe. Occasional finds are still a possibility, but systematic 78rpm collecting must nowadays make use of the established means of exchange.

According to Stephen Smith, in *Jazzmen*, the earliest known collectors were four members of Princeton University, followed closely by a group at Yale which included the well known names of Wilder Hobson and John Hammond. Charles Edward Smith, joint editor of *Jazzmen*, was influenced by the Princeton group and persuaded to write an article on collecting. It was published in *Esquire* in 1934 and was the first piece of publicity for the activity.

To understand what collecting was like in those days (approximately 1925-1935) we have to imagine a time when the history of the music had not been explored, when there were no books as guides and above all no discographies. The early collector's knowledge was hard-earned, but he did have the exciting prospect of finding previously unknown recordings. The best picture of this state of affairs was drawn by Ernest Borneman in an article entitled 'The jazz cult', which was first published in *Harper's magazine* in 1947 and reprinted in Eddie Condon's *Treasury of jazz*.

From 1935 to 1945 there was some expansion in jazz collecting, occasioned largely by the publicity attending the big swing bands. But, as anyone who started collecting in that period knows, it was comparatively rare to meet anyone with a similar interest and the majority of people were unaware of the distinction between jazz and popular music. The end of the war marks the boundary between the ancient and modern history of jazz collecting. An article on 'Jazz and the collector', by Thurman and

Mary Grove, was included in the booklet *Jazz review,* published by Jazz Music Books in 1945. It is an excellent summary of this first period of jazz collecting.

## THE PSYCHOLOGY OF RECORD LENGTH

The restrictive effect of the three minute record has been remarked by more than one writer on jazz. Certainly musicians were used to improvising at greater length, and certainly one can think of records that seem to break off too soon. The outstanding example of this that comes to my mind is Dicky Wells' ' Japanese Sandman ' from the 1937 Paris session. The last chorus is particularly fine, but instead of acting as a climax to the performance it gives promise of at least three more minutes to come. The musicians are abruptly stopped in full flight and one has the feeling that the high spot of the whole session was lost. A rare example of the older musician improvising at length in a ' live ' performance is the remarkable 16 chorus solo by John Handy on ' Jazz crusade ' JC 2008. On the whole the time limit was probably more gain than loss. It acted as a discipline which saved us from the longueurs of many later recordings on LP. A very interesting analysis of one way in which the limit was turned to positive advantage was made by Martin Williams in his essay ' Recording limits and the blues form '.

Apart from its effect on the music, record length also has relevance to the listener. In *Dinosaurs in the morning,* Whitney Balliett suggests that ' Perhaps the chief appeal of genuine jazz improvisation lies in its ability to supply the listener in a matter of moments with an emotional and aesthetic sustenance comparable to that provided by the heavier arts—a peculiarly valuable ability in this split-second age '. The word ' comparable ' has questionable implications, but I think there is a great deal of truth in this view.

Even since the abolition of the restriction imposed by the 78rpm record, the length of individual jazz performances has remained short in comparison with classical music. But whereas on 78s one performance corresponded to one side of a record, an LP side contains several performances. The 12 inch LP has become the commonest medium both for new jazz and for reissues. In the United States it is now the only form, and even in European countries only the small specialist companies now issue 45rpm and $33\frac{1}{3}$rpm 7 inch discs. The 10 inch LP is also obsolete, but in the early days of microgroove many reissues appeared in this form.

The greatest advantage of the 12 inch LP is in its value for money. For technical reasons it is not always the best form. Modern recordings are made with this length in mind and performances are adjusted to it, just as they were to the 78. But simply because they were condensed into three minute performances, these early recordings are often better heard in shorter doses than the 25 minutes of an LP side. Furthermore, there were many recording sessions of 4 performances which fit admirably the 45rpm format. Listening psychology and availability of time both warrant the existence of different record sizes.

The modern collection is likely to include all the forms mentioned, since even the 10 inch LP is still available in the second-hand market. But the 12 inch LP will usually predominate, and for this reason it is worthwhile having a pickup with a lowering device. Individual tracks can then be played as desired. It is not advisable to try this without such a device as it is difficult to do so without damaging the record.

SPECIALIZATION IN CLASSICS

The only completely general collection worth building is one based on selection of the best of every style. In one way it is the easiest form of specialization, since by and large there is more chance of classics being easily available than lesser performances. In another way it is the most difficult since it demands extensive knowledge and judgment. There are a number of published guides to help here and they will be discussed later (pages 52-3).

For the private collector this is the least likely form of specialization since there are few people who do not have strong preferences for certain styles and certain artists. For libraries it should be the standard method. I disagree with an opinion expressed by a librarian, J B Coover, in the *Library journal*, May 15 1956. His argument was that purchases should be limited to performances of historical significance and influence as it was too early to make esthetic judgments. Admittedly this was written over 10 years ago, but recorded jazz was nearly forty years old even then. If one cannot make judgments after 40 years how long does one have to wait? If this view were valid one would expect to find more disagreement among critics than is normal in the arts. In fact, one finds the usual arguments as to the relative values of different styles, and the usual agreement as to what is good within any one of them.

SPECIALIZATION BY STYLE

In 1965 Charles Fox gave one of the best series of talks on jazz ever broadcast by the BBC. He distinguished between jazz as functional music, as entertainment and as art. These are not mutually exclusive categories and some jazz has elements of all three. But if we use the predominating element as the criterion of distinction, this tripartite division of jazz is a useful one and corresponds partly to the more technical terms, traditional, mainstream and modern. Technical distinctions are important for some purposes, but they are always secondary. Our ultimate concern is *what* the music does, not *how* it does it.

The finest analysis of the nature of jazz published so far is in Wilfrid Mellers' *Music in a new found land*. Jazz is placed here in its context of American music as a whole, and the interweaving of the functional, entertainment and art threads is carefully examined.

Many people like all forms of jazz, but they do not get the same kind of experience from each. The following sections provide a few comments on the nature of these different experiences.

JAZZ AS FUNCTIONAL (OR FOLK) MUSIC

If ' folk ' is used to imply rural and unprofessional, then only the forms of Afro-American music that preceded jazz qualify for the description. Comparatively few records have been made of those forms, which include work songs, spirituals, gospel songs and primitive blues. The rural-unprofessional distinction does more or less account for work songs, but gospel songs continue to be sung in town churches. Spirituals have been absorbed into western art music in the way that European folk songs have. It is for the blues that the distinction has least significance. They are still very much alive in an urban/professional form, and though there are considerable differences between, say, Blind Lemon Jefferson, Bessie Smith and Jimmy Witherspoon, there is a spirit common to all three. The same spirit is to be found in the sophisticated music of Duke Ellington, and this makes it possible to talk of the folk element in jazz, even though it has never been folk music in a strict sense.

The 'functional' characteristic, used by Charles Fox, is more useful than 'rural/unprofessional' since it emphasizes the essence of early jazz as the social music of a particular group of people. Apart from the song forms already mentioned it would include the marching bands, the dance bands and blues piano playing. Many of the jazz recordings of the 'twenties and 'thirties were produced just for the Negro market, and known as race records. They included many blues singers accompanied by jazz musicians, boogie-woogie pianists, and small dance bands typified by the south side Chicago groups made up of musicians like Johnny Dodds and Natty Dominique. It was simple, rough, earthy music, at the furthest extreme from western art music. Herein lies its attraction to the sophisticated and intellectual contemporary.

In an urban environment a folk music cannot for long retain its original simplicity, owing to the influence of other kinds of music. However, the functional dance music *is* still played in various towns of the United States, even if it hasn't been much recorded since the 'twenties. An example is Junie Cobb's Hometown Band in the Riverside 'Chicago: the living legends' series. It obviously shows some influence of later jazz, but this spirit is similar to that of the Chicago South Side music of the 'twenties. 'The legendary Buster Smith' (Am Atlantic 1323), recorded in Texas, is much more modern but, apart from Smith's alto, consists largely of functional riffing. As Gunther Schuller explains in his notes on the record, 'To Buster, jazz has had to mean strictly functional dance music. Solid rocking rhythms to which people can dance are far more important in Buster's everyday existence than melody or inventive improvisations *per se.*'

Any discussion of jazz as folk music must give special attention to the music of New Orleans. Whatever the truth about its place in the creation of jazz, New Orleans is certainly unique in the length of time for which it retained a distinctive style of functional music. Regional styles were not very distinct even in the earliest days of jazz recording and by the mid 'thirties they could hardly be said to exist. From the evidence of records, however, the music of New Orleans has always had a distinctive flavour of its own. Very few recordings were made there before the 'forties,

31

but the bands of Oscar Celestin, Louis Dumaine and Sam Morgan do not sound like anything recorded in Chicago or New York during the same period. The Jones and Collins sides of 1929 admittedly sound similar to the Luis Russell band under Henry Allen's leadership, but Samuel Charters explains that they were the only recordings made by ' young men in the city who had grown up in the city's tradition, and then listened to the Chicago musicians '. The many recordings made in New Orleans since 1940 all have a character which mark them off from traditional bands elsewhere. It is significant that the George Lewis band, which subsequently travelled around and recorded extensively, developed a much more general ' dixieland ' sound.

Many criticisms of New Orleans music are invalid because they use the wrong criteria. It must be seen as a form of near-folk music and judged accordingly. New Orleans provides an experience unique in jazz and a good subject for specialization. Despite its neglect by major record companies, the music has been well served by enthusiasts in the last twenty five years. Samuel Charters was responsible both for the guide, *Jazz: New Orleans 1885-1963,* and for the Folkways anthology of recordings (FA 2461-5) which includes street cries, brass bands, religious singers and mardi gras music, as well as regular traditional dance hall bands. Other notable series were the American Music recordings of the 'forties, the Riverside ' New Orleans: the living legends ' and the Icons, both of the 'sixties. This decade has seen a remarkable growth of small companies specializing in New Orleans music, such as Mono, GHB, Center, Pearl, Jazz Crusade, Jazzology and San Jacinto. New Orleans has its own Jazz Museum and its own magazine, *The second line,* published by the New Orleans Jazz Club. An English Magazine, *Eureka,* which was devoted to New Orleans music, lasted for just over a year in 1960. *New Orleans jazz: a family album,* by Al Rose and Edmond Souchon, is one of the best jazz reference books yet published, and certainly the finest collection of photographs.

JAZZ AS ENTERTAINMENT

In *Jazz: a history of the New York scene,* by Sam Charters and Len Kunstadt, jazz is referred to as ' an uneasy compromise between the folk music of the American Negro and the popular music of the white population '. This won't do as a general definition of jazz, but it does point to a characteristic of the new style that developed in the 'thirties which is at least as important as the technical changes of the time. The significance of the themes used for improvisation has not received a great deal of attention in the writings on jazz. Leroy Ostransky, in *The anatomy of jazz,* treats them as one element in the definition of styles, but the fullest treatment of their place in jazz is given by Sidney Finkelstein in *Jazz: a people's music.* The effect of the theme can easily be judged by comparing the performances of a popular song and a jazz composition by any dixieland group (*eg* ' I guess I'll have to change my plan ' and ' Muskrat ramble ' by Bobby Hackett on REG 2062).

American popular music, even at its best, is rarely free of sentimentality. Interested readers will find a good discussion in S I Hayakawa's ' Popular songs vs the facts of life ' in *Our language and our world* (Harper, 1959). In Oscar Wilde's excellent definition ' a sentimentalist is simply one who desires to have the luxury of an emotion without paying for it '. Luxuries without payment are a common enough objective in our day, but few are as damaging as this one. A common way of correcting any bad tendency in society is humour, and Fats Waller is the outstanding example of a jazzman using this method of dealing with the mediocre popular songs of his time. The novelty band of Spike Jones and his City Slickers performed a similar service, one of their best records being ' You always hurt the one you love '. The melody of this song is poor and the words beyond redemption. Even the great Jimmy Rushing could do nothing with them in his 1963 recording (' Five feet of soul ', Colpix CP446). Without the benefit of jazz, Spike Jones' treatment leads to complete destruction of the song. But when words are beyond redemption, jazzmen can salvage something from the melody. In Bunk Johnson's recording (Storyville SEP401), the edgy bitter sound of the New Orleans ensemble brings reality and distinction in place of sentimentality and banality.

Tin Pan Alley songs are not usually just nonsense. They deal with important matters, but without any distinction of language and with a tendency to wallow in the emotions. One can often find a similar theme, realistically treated, in literature. For example, we might compare ' You always hurt the one you love ' with a stanza from Oscar Wilde's *Ballad of Reading Gaol:*

33

2

Yet each man kills the thing he loves,
By each let this be heard,
Some do it with a bitter look,
Some with a flattering word,
The coward does it with a kiss,
The brave man with a sword.

*You always hurt the one you love,*
*The one you shouldn't hurt at all.*
*You always take the sweetest rose*
*And crush it till the petals fall . . .*
*So if I broke your heart last night*
*It's because I love you most of all.*

A better song is ' I cried for you ', but its words are hardly distinguished.

*I cried for you, now it's your turn to cry over me*
*Every road has its turning*
*That's one thing you're learning*
*I cried for you, now it's your turn to cry over me.*

*I cried for you, what a fool I used to be*
*Now I've found two eyes just a little bit bluer*
*I've found a heart just a little bit truer*
*I cried for you, now it's your turn to cry over me.*

We might compare this first with a modern blues treatment of the same theme, ' The feeling is gone ' as sung by Bobby Bland and included in Charles Keil's *The urban blues:*

*When I needed you to stand by my side*
*All you did was laugh while I cried.*
*And now you want me to take you back in my arms*
*Oh-oooo-oh, it's too late, baby*
*I'm here to tell you that the feelin' is gone.*

*I remember the look on your face,*
*Ooow, when you told me that I was being replaced.*
*Now you're beggin' me, you say you wanna come back home.*
*Oh-oooo-oh, it's too late baby*
*I'm standin' here to tell you that the feelin' is gone.*

34

*You told me to hit the road, and I did just that.*
*Now you find out that you need me, but ooh, I ain't comin' back.*
*And now you say you want me to take you back in my arms*
*Oh-oooo-oh, I say it's too late baby*
*Loooooord, I tell you the feelin' is gone.*

The most distinguished treatment of the theme is to be found in Thomas Carew's ' To his inconstant mistress ':

When thou, poore excommunicate
   From all the joyes of love, shalt see
The full reward, the glorious fate,
   Which my strong faith shall purchase me,
Then curse thine owne inconstancy.

A fayrer hand than thine, shall cure
   That heart, which thy false oathes did wound;
And to my soul, a soul more pure
   Than thine, shall by Loves hand be bound,
And both with equall glory crown'd.

Then shalt thou weepe, entreat, complain
   To Love, as I did once to thee;
When all thy teares shall be as vain
   As mine were then, for thou shalt bee
Damn'd for thy false Apostasie.

It requires experience as well as technical facility to write with this intensity. The jazz singer requires a similar combination. This is common enough among blues singers, but extremely rare in singers of popular songs. The technical difficulty is well analysed by Benny Green in his essay on Billie Holiday in *The reluctant art*. In fact, Billie Holiday is the only singer with these qualities. It is instructive to compare her recording of ' I cried for you ' with Ella Fitzgerald's. The latter is a high class piece of light entertainment, but it has no emotional power. Billie Holiday's performance is in a different class. Her ability to recreate the melody and to infuse the banal words with her own experience result in a song which does belong to the same level of experience as Carew's poem. Childhood is a theme in which it is extremely difficult to avoid sentimentality. Poets sometimes walk the tightrope, as D H Lawrence does in ' Piano '. Popular song writers always fall off. Hoagy Carmichael's 'Mandy is two' is a typical example. Nothing is stronger evidence of Billie Holiday's genius than her recording of this song which transmutes the maudlin material into one of her most moving performances.

Discussions on what constitutes popular music never seem to reach a firm conclusion. Perhaps Ted Hughes expressed the essence when he observed, in a *Guardian* review of *The Faber book of ballads*, that 'human beings are at the mercy of unforgettable melodies'. Unfortunately, a melody needn't be good to be unforgettable. For the last fifty years the world has been increasingly at the mercy of the melodies created by Tin Pan Alley. A small proportion are good and unforgettable; many are poor and easily forgettable. In between are a vast number which are unforgettable but flagrantly sentimental.

Sentimentality is a highly significant factor in modern civilization. Material progress and success in controlling nature have led to a prevailing Utopian philosophy. The essence of modern consumer advertising is Utopian imagery, against which the immature have no defence. It is nice to believe in such a world, and the easy conditions of middle class life predispose many people to do so. Very few of them can complete their lives without a rude awakening. As Yeats said, 'We begin to live when we have conceived life as tragedy'. People who live in hard conditions are not prone to sentimentality: the Negro folk music that provided the heart of jazz was never sentimental. For a large number of modern people there is a poignant conflict, and it seems to me that the attraction of a great deal of jazz lies in its symbolization of this conflict. The Utopian dream is represented by the sentimental melody and it is balanced by the vitality of artists who create a reality with their improvisations.

An analysis of one recording will serve to demonstrate the point. Jimmie Noone's 'Every Evening' (I miss you) has always had a strong appeal for me, which I could never explain until I analysed it in these terms. After the introduction, based on the verse of the song, there are four choruses. In the first, the melody is carried by the sweet, cloying tones of the alto while Noone plays exciting variations on the clarinet, which breaks through the alto lead like flashes of reality interrupting a daydream. Chorus two by Hines' piano prepares for a change of roles. Noone takes the lead in chorus three while the alto's melody appears spasmodically in the background—suggesting that even when reality gets the upper hand it is impossible to eliminate the daydream completely. The final chorus is a battle between clarinet and alto, the clarinet having sufficiently the better of the argument to provide a satisfactory resolution of the tension in favour of the creative reality.

Some popular songs are not sentimental, but light-hearted and humorous. A similar balancing of original melody and improvisation can be used here to point the contrast between the ordinary and the distinguished. My favourite example is Red Nichols' ' Sheik of Araby '. Twice on this record, Jack Teagarden gives such a demonstration. The first is explicit, when he breaks into the corny vocal to replace it with his own distinctive and felicitous manner. The second is implicit. After the vocal, Glenn Miller begins a sweet, soft solo. Teagarden leaves him just enough time to establish the melody before superimposing one of his finest improvisations. The duet is effective and enchanting. This performance can stand as the epitome of entertainment jazz.

## JAZZ AS ART

The term ' art ' is used here in the restricted sense of the more complex forms characteristic of highly developed cultures. The earlier periods of jazz were not without their artists in this sense, and due credit has been given to Jelly Roll Morton and Duke Ellington. It is only in the modern period, however, that we can see this ' artistic ' element predominating.

The appeal of modern jazz is very different from that of the forms so far discussed. It is often created in the spirit of a concert-hall music rather than a popular music. In so far as it uses the blues as theme it retains something of the original folk element. In so far as it uses popular songs it preserves nothing of their original quality. The peculiar tension between original melody and recreation that is a fundamental feature of much mainstream jazz no longer exists in modern. Its affinity is much more with modern art music than with popular music. More of its musicians are trained rather than self-taught, and influenced by the techniques and developments in classical music. The uneasy compromise between the folk music of the American negro and the popular music of the white population has been succeeded by two tendencies. One is towards a compromise with European classical music, as in 'progressive' jazz and Third Stream, the other is towards the establishment of a 'pure' black music that can stand comparison with the achievements of the European tradition. This second tendency began with the Bop movement of the 'forties, which deliberately shunned the popular elements of the swing period, and has become far more radical with the current avant garde. This is certainly the most self-conscious phase of jazz and for the present it is difficult to separate its lasting musical value from its immediate social significance (see *Black music* by Le Roi Jones and the review by Philip Larkin in the *Guardian*, September 4, 1969).

Despite these modern developments, some people would still see Duke Ellington's music as the peak of jazz art. Certainly it is unique in the way that it combines folk, popular and art elements.

### SPECIALIZATION BY BANDS AND MUSICIANS

Within any of the major styles of jazz most collectors have their favourite bands and musicians. Such preference forms the commonest base of specialization and also provides the feasibility of completing a series. The difficulty of this will vary according to the extent of the musician's recordings and their rarity. In most cases there will be at least a few performances that are difficult to obtain. This, of course, merely adds to the zest of the search and the satisfaction of reaching the objective. It provides a typical ingredient of the collecting activity. Discographies have the same importance here as bibliographies for the book collector. They will be discussed in the next chapter.

### SPECIALIZATION BY TUNES

Though the basic theme is not the most important element in jazz it is not without its effect. Compositions of musicians such as Duke Ellington and Jelly Roll Morton have a value of their own, and a collection of such a musician's recordings may well be extended to include recordings of his tunes by other musicians. Many themes of folk jazz are very beautiful and a complete collection of recordings of 'Careless love' or 'Trouble in mind', for example, would be a worthwhile objective. I suppose most collectors also have soft spots for certain popular songs, good or indifferent. In this case selective collecting is called for, but it is the one instance where even the purest jazz man is likely to relax his principles and let in some good examples from the other side of the pop/jazz border.

It is hard work compiling a list of recordings of a particular tune, since none of the general discographies has a tune index. Separate discographies of the most important would be useful, but very few have ever appeared in magazines.

PLANNING A JAZZ RECORD COLLECTION

Those who want to be in the fashion buy a new car every year, and regard depreciation as the price of satisfying their taste. Casual jazz fans may have the same attitude to records. The collector has a very different objective and, in England at any rate, cannot afford very much chance buying. There is more scope in America, where records are cheaper in relation to incomes, discount selling is widespread, and sales are frequent.

The collector's knowledge is acquired by a mixture of reading and listening. Reading will be dealt with in the next chapter. All that needs to be said about listening is that it is the only way of finding out what you like. Since buying for this purpose is not economically desirable, other means must be used. Jazz clubs, radio and friends' collections are all useful, but the best method is borrowing records from libraries. Provision of jazz records in public libraries is not yet adequate, but it is steadily increasing. If you live in an area where it is non-existent or unsatisfactory you should press for improvement.

When it comes to buying, the best sources are the specialist jazz dealers, including a few general shops with good jazz departments. Their advantage is not only in knowledge of the records, but also in the scope of their stock. The chief problem for the collector is the rapid and frequent deletion of records. At any one time in any one country, the records in print constitute only a small proportion of the whole. The specialists give the best possible service by importing from all over the world and also by dealing in secondhand copies.

Careful planning is especially called for in the buying of reissues. Owing to the unsystematic nature of most of them, there is considerable overlapping between different countries and even between issues in one country at different times. For example, recordings by Johnny Dodds have appeared in many different forms. They have included 10 inch and 12 inch LPs on American Riverside, 10 inch LPs on English London, 10 inch LPs and EPs on English HMV and French RCA, EPS on German Coral, and 7 inch LPs on Australian Swaggie. The Dodds collector would be well advised to make a complete survey before buying anything. Otherwise, he may easily spend twice as much money as he need to complete the collection. In buying reissues it is very difficult to avoid at least some duplication, and in most cases probably impossible. But planning can reduce it to a minimum. The knowledge necessary to effect such planning is an important part of the collector's skill. It forms the subject of the next chapter.

The last paragraph of this chapter is reserved for the most important piece of advice. Don't be in a hurry to sell anything you have once liked. In the early years of collecting, at least, interests are likely to fluctuate. Later experiences may temporarily obliterate earlier ones, but the chances of revival are high. Nearly everything I have sold in the past I have wanted to replace later. At the best this is a waste of money; at the worst it is the risk of having great difficulty in finding the replacement.

READINGS FOR CHAPTER ONE

(Publications are English unless otherwise stated.)

1 *Collecting in general*

Cabanne, Pierre: *The great collectors.* Cassell, 1964.

Carter, John: *Taste and technique in book collecting.* Cambridge University Press, 1948.

Chapman, R W: 'The sense of the past'. *Book collectors' quarterly,* June/August, 1931, pp 48-63.

Clark, Sir Kenneth: 'The great private collectors'. *Sunday times colour magazine,* September 22 1963, pp 14-26.

Jackson, Holbrook: *The anatomy of bibliomania.* Faber, 1950.

Lucie-Smith, Edward: Introduction to *Poetry catalogue.* Bertram Rota, Summer 1966.

Powys, John Cowper: *The art of happiness.* John Lane, 1935, pp 195-196.

Rigby, Douglas & Elizabeth: *Lock, stock and barrel: the story of collecting.* Philadelphia, J B Lippincott, 1944 (includes 15 page bibliography).

Whitehorn, Katherine: ' Magpies '. *Spectator,* October 5 1962 pp 537-8.

## 2 *Record collecting*

Bryant, E T: *Collecting gramophone records.* Focal Press, 1962.

Currall, F J (*ed*): *Gramophone record libraries: their organization and practice.* Crosby Lockwood, 1963 (second edition to be published in 1970).

Hurst, P G: *The golden age recorded: a collector's survey.* The Author, 1946.

Hall, David: ' The collectors organize '. *Hi fi/stereo review,* New York, March 1967, pp 44, 46.

Johnson, William W: *The gramophone book: a complete guide for all lovers of recorded music.* Hinrichsen Editions, 1954.

March, Ivan: *Running a record library.* LP Record Library, 1965.

Menuhin, Yehudi & Keller, Hans: 'Are records musical?' *Audio and record review,* March and April 1966. (Reprinted in *Hi fi/stereo review,* New York, February 1967.)

Overton, C D: *The gramophone record library.* Grafton, 1951.

Robertson, Alec: ' The record collector '. *Penguin music magazine* I, December 1946, pp 90-94.

Semeonoff, Boris: *Record collecting: a guide for beginners.* Oakwood Press, second edition, 1951.

Wilson, Colin: *Brandy of the damned.* John Baker, 1964. (Published in USA as *Chords and discords.* New York, Crown Publishers, 1966.)

## 3 *Jazz collecting*

Allen. Walter C: ' Original labels '. *Jazz journal.* October 1956.

Anderson, A: *Helpful hints to jazz collectors.* Baraboo, Wisconsin, Andoll, 1957.

Balliett, Whitney: *Dinosaurs in the morning.* Phoenix House, 1964. Title essay.

Borneman, Ernest: ' The jazz cult '. *Harper's magazine* (USA), 1947, pp 141-7, 261-273. Reprinted in Condon, E & Gehman, R (*eds*): *Eddie Condon's treasury of jazz.* Peter Davies, 1957.

Carey, Dave: ' Young collectors' guide to other collectors '. *Jazz journal,* June 1949.

41

2*

Clarke, Gray & Davis, John: 'The agelasts'. *Jazz music,* vol 4 no 1.

Coover, James B: ' Basic jazz collection '. *Library journal* (USA), May 15 1956.

DeToledano, R *(ed)*: *Frontiers of jazz.* Oliver Durrell, 1947. Introduction.

Ertegun, Marili: 'The anatomy of discomania'. *Jazzfinder* (USA), April & November 1948.

Ertegun, Marili: ' Collecting hot 1927-1947 '. *Record changer* (USA), October 1947.

Ferguson, Otis: ' Records: a start on jazz '. *New republic* (USA), February 9 1942.

Gleason, Ralph J: 'A short analysis of hot jazz record collecting'. *Hobbies* (USA), May 1941.

Grauer, Bill: ' Collecting hot since '42 '. *Record changer* (USA), August/September 1952.

Grauer, Bill: ' In defense of label collecting'. *Record changer* (USA), May 1950.

Grossman, William L and Farrell, Jack W: *The heart of jazz.* Vision Press, 1958. Chapter 32 ' The jazz record collector '.

Grove, Thurman & Mary: ' Jazz and the collector'. In *Jazz review.* Jazz Music Books, 1945.

Hoefer, George: ' Collectors: Personalities and anecdotes '. In *Esquire's jazz book. New York,* Smith & Durrell, 1944. (Reprinted in *Esquire's jazz book.* Peter Davies, 1947).

Hoefer, George: ' Wartime hints for collectors '. In *Esquire's 1945 jazz book.* New York, A S Barnes, 1945.

Hoefer, George: ' The collectors' outlook '. In *Esquire's 1946 jazz book.* New York, A S Barnes, 1946.

James, Burnett: *Living forwards.* Cassell, 1961.

Newton, Francis: *The jazz scene.* Penguin, 1961.

Ramsey, Frederic: ' Discollecting'. In Rosenthal, G S *(ed):* *Jazzways.* New York, Greenberg, 1947.

Ross, Alexander: ' Collecting jazz records '. In Semeonoff, B : *Record collecting.* Oakwood Press, second edition 1951.

Smith, Charles Edward: ' Collecting hot'. *Esquire* (USA), February 1934. (Reprinted in *Esquire's jazz book.* New York, Smith & Durrell, 1944 and *Esquire's jazz book.* Peter Davies, 1947.)

Smith, Charles Edward: ' Collecting hot'. *Esquire* (USA), February 1944.

Smith, Charles Edward: ' Background to bootlegging '. *Record changer* (USA), January 1952.

Smith, Stephen: ' Hot collecting '. In Ramsey, F & Smith, C E *(eds)*: *Jazzmen*. Sidgwick & Jackson, 1957.

Stearns, Marshall: ' Collecting jazz: 1958 '. *Esquire* (USA), February 1958.

Williams, Martin: ' Recording limits and blues form '. In Williams, M *(ed)*: *The art of jazz*. Cassell, 1960.

## 4 Jazz styles and popular music

Charters, Samuel B: *Jazz: New Orleans, 1885-1963*. New York, Oak Publications, second edition 1963.

Dachs, David: *Anything goes : the world of popular music*. New York, Bobbs-Merrill, 1964.

Finkelstein, S: *Jazz: a people's music*. New York, Citadel Press, 1948.

Green, Benny: *The reluctant art: five studies in the growth of jazz*. MacGibbon & Kee, 1962. Essay on Billie Holiday.

Hayakawa, S I: ' Popular songs vs the facts of life '. In Hayakawa, S I *(ed)*: *Our language and our world*. New York, Harper, 1959.

Hodeir, A: *Jazz: its evolution and essence*. Secker & Warburg, 1956.

James, Burnett: ' Viewpoint: 28 '. *Audio record review*, November 1969 (on jazz influence in European music).

Jones, Le Roi: *Black music*. New York, Morrow, 1968.

Mellers, Wilfrid: *Music in a new found land*. Barrie and Rockliff, 1963.

Ostransky, Leroy: *The anatomy of jazz*. Seattle, University of Washington Press, 1960.

# *The collector's aids*

The collector differs from the casually interested person, not only in his systematic buying, but also in his desire to know everything about his chosen subject. The main sources for the jazz collector are books and periodicals, but there are also a few relevant institutions. They are of two kinds: those for the performance of jazz, and those for its preservation. They are not entirely distinct but may be treated so for convenience.

INSTITUTIONS FOR THE PERFORMANCE OF JAZZ

Though it looks like a distortion of values, there are several reasons for treating live performance as subordinate to gramophone records. In this book we are talking about collecting, which in itself relegates live performance to a secondary position. We are talking about all jazz, past and present, of which live performance represents a diminishing proportion. We are talking about collectors, many of whom would share Colin Wilson's preference for home listening. In addition we must remember that only in a few cities of the United States has there ever been the opportunity for frequent listening to a good range of jazz styles. We are not here concerned with the intrinsic value of live performance, but with its value for those who listen mainly to records. It is generally agreed that the imagination can at least partly supply what is missing even in poor quality recordings. Imagination feeds on memory, and it is memory of live performance that serves as a valuable aid to the record collector.

Each of the main forms of jazz—functional, entertainment, art—has its own appropriate institution for performance. In the earliest days, in certain parts of the United States, any social function served as a medium for jazz, but this condition now exists only in an attenuated form in New Orleans. There has been some European imitation as, for example, in the accompaniment

44

to protest marches. The one universal institution for functional jazz is the dance hall, and the corresponding institution for entertainment and art are the night club and concert hall respectively. Each form suffers from performance in the wrong setting. For the sake of the musicians it is good that Preservation Hall and Dixieland Hall exist, but they are a great disappointment to the New Orleans pilgrim. The music cries out for dancing participators not for seated spectators. If you are looking for the spirit of King Oliver you will come much closer by taking the floor in any negro dance hall purveying modern ' Soul ' music. Henry Allen on stage during an English tour was impressive, but it needed the more intimate atmosphere of a night club to reveal the full effect of his personality and music.

Two further institutions should be suitable for any kind of jazz. Jazz (or rhythm) clubs have existed since the 'twenties, though before the war they were mainly places to hear, buy or exchange records and to learn something about jazz from those who had a longer acquaintance. They can still be valuable in these ways, but it is much easier now than it was then to learn about the music by reading. For live performances a club is free to alter conditions to suit the type of music. Festivals have grown up during the last fifteen years. Potentially they have the flexibility of the club, but in practice have been more like the concert hall than anything else. They suffer from the infrequent, big occasion atmosphere in which the quality of performance is a matter of luck.

INSTITUTIONS FOR THE PRESERVATION OF JAZZ

The 1958 Newport Festival is preserved in the film *Jazz on a summer's day*. Many other performances are preserved as incidental or background music to films. A good jazz history or biography on film has yet to be made; but there are some entertaining stories with a jazz theme, good music and screen appearances of real musicians. *The birth of the blues, Syncopation* and *Paris blues* are examples. More important are the short feature films and documentaries that have been made since the 'twenties. These are less accessible than general films, and once again we owe to private collectors our knowledge of their existence. A good survey of jazz on film was written by Dan Morgenstern for the 1967 *Downbeat yearbook*.

There are still very few organizations whose sole purpose is the preservation, study and dissemination of jazz. The oldest and most comprehensive is the Institute of Jazz Studies. It was founded in 1952 by Marshall Stearns and since his death in 1966 has been taken over by Rutgers University. The collection includes some 17,000 records, as well as piano rolls, cylinders, tapes, musical instruments etc. According to its secretary, Sheldon Harris, it also includes nearly every book published on jazz and related subjects. His short account of the institute and its activities appeared in *Jazz journal,* June 1963.

New Orleans has two organizations. The Jazz Museum was founded in 1961 and contains about 10,000 items relating to jazz history—including the carriage stone from Mahogany Hall, which must be one of the very few traces of Storyville left in existence. The assistant curator in regular attendance is guitarist Danny Barker, whose forthcoming book on New Orleans will almost certainly be the most important yet published. The New Orleans Archive was established at Tulane University in 1958 with the aid of a Ford Foundation grant. Its curator, Richard Allen, wrote an account of its activities for the Oral History Symposium published in *Wilson library bulletin,* March 1966. Oral history is the most important of these activities, and by 1967 the Archive had put over 500 interviews on tape. The collection also includes some 11,000 records, piano rolls, sheet music, films, nearly 5,000 books and periodicals, over 4,000 photographs, and nearly 3,000 items relating to Nick La Rocca and the Original Dixieland Jazz Band.

There is no English organization that can at present compare in size or scope with these. The British Institute of Jazz Studies, founded in 1964, is compiling a comprehensive index of musicians and collecting literature and records. It also issues a periodical called *Jazz studies.* A brief account can be found in the February 1969 issue of *Jazz monthly.*

Of general organizations whose interests include jazz the most important is the Library of Congress. The work of John and Alan Lomax for the archive of folk-song is well known, including the invaluable story of Jelly Roll Morton recorded in 1938. I know of no library in England with a good collection of jazz literature or records.

The International Association of Jazz Record Collectors was

founded in 1964, with headquarters in Pittsburgh. Its objectives are described in *Storyville* no 21.

Another useful development in America was the formation of the Association for Recorded Sound Collections. In his article for *Hi fi/stereo review*, March 1967, David Hall reported that at least half of those present for the inaugural meeting were private collectors. He described the proposed objectives of the association as collecting information about record libraries and collections throughout the world, compiling a union catalogue, making recordings available through channels including commercial companies and audition facilities in libraries, and taping rare materials for the use of scholars. The first project was to be a directory of important institutional and private collections in the United States and Canada, with the hope that it would later be expanded to include the whole world.

Institutions for preserving jazz may be classified as primary or secondary. Secondary organizations can collect only what primary organizations have produced. I began by mentioning films, but the major primary organizations are, of course, the record companies. What is easily available now and what will be in the future are dependent on their policies. The history of companies, their archives and catalogues are all important sources of information. Before the comprehensive discographies of jazz could be produced it was necessary to identify all the recording companies concerned and to obtain complete lists of their output. We certainly know about the vast majority of recordings made in the past, but it is still likely that diligent research will produce hitherto unknown items, as well as further information about known items. There is no comprehensive history of the jazz record companies, but in *A glimpse at the past* Michael Wyler produced a valuable account of the most important small companies operating in the earliest days. The same author's listing of the Paramount 12000-13000 series was published in issues of the first five volumes of *Jazz monthly*. Other articles on early companies and lists of their records have appeared in various jazz magazines. A good example is the 'Perfect Dance and Race Catalogue 1922-1930', by Carl Kendziora and Percy Armagnac, which occupied the whole of one issue of *Record research* (May/June 1963). An example of a separately published label discography is *The Columbia 13/14000—D series*, by Dan Mahony.

Apart from the few institutions already mentioned, most research in jazz has been conducted by private individuals. As the results have mainly appeared in ordinary commercial publications I shall include them in the next section, on the literature of jazz. The one aspect deserving special attention is discography. Field research began rather late in the day, since the Americans were behind Europeans in recognising the importance of jazz. If we must regret the irrevocable loss, we must also rejoice at the inevitable direction taken by European research. Discography is by far the most important aid to the jazz collector. One can no more be a jazz collector without discographies than one can be a book collector without bibliographies. (I have seen more than one writer apologise for 'discography' as an ugly and hybrid word. In fact it is no hybrid but of classical construction, like bibliography. It is certainly not an ugly word to me—austere, perhaps.) Both activities are labours of love, calling for arduous and painstaking work with little financial reward. It says much for the fascination of jazz that it has inspired so much work of this kind. An outstanding English discographer, Albert McCarthy, estimated in 1964 that there were well over 100 active jazz discographers in the world. The task itself may be hard, but the results are a joy to the real collector. One test of the real collector is the enthusiasm with which he welcomes a new discography, and the pleasure he derives from studying its pages. It is easy to make fun of 'Scholars manqués . . . wrapped up in personnels like old plaids', as Philip Larkin describes them in his poem 'For Sidney Bechet'. No form of scholarship is without such dangers, and jazz probably has its share of characters who become absorbed in means at the expense of ends. We mustn't allow this fact to obscure the true value of the work.

Jazz discography began in 1936 with the publication of Hilton Schleman's *Rhythm on record* in England and Charles Delaunay's *Hot discography* in France. Schleman's book was far less influential than Delaunay's and is now a rare collector's item. *Hot discography* went through several editions and was for many years the jazz collector's *vade mecum*. The last complete edition was that of 1948: a later revision in several volumes failed to get beyond the letter H. By the end of the war jazz had ceased to be an esoteric subject. As output increased, particularly after the introduction of LPs, it become progressively more difficult for discographers to keep pace. The very fine *Jazz directory*, by Dave Carey and Albert McCarthy, suffered a similar fate to that of *Hot discography*. Between 1949 and 1957 it reached the letter L and there, to the great sorrow of collectors, it ended. A further attempt by Albert McCarthy to deal with the output year by year also failed, only one volume, entitled *Jazz discography 1958*, being published. The first and, so far, only general discography by an American appeared in four volumes between 1945 and 1948 with the title *Index to jazz*. The author, Orin Blackstone, described this first edition in his *Jazzfinder '49* as a 'rough draft'. The definitive edition, embodying corrections and additions from collectors all over the world, began in 1949. That too failed to see completion, only the first volume being published.

These four works are the great pioneers of jazz discography. Collectors whose interest extends to the literature will want to own copies for this reason alone, but their value is not merely historical. In the first place it is difficult to draw a clear line between jazz and 'hot' dance music, or between jazz and other forms of Afro-American music. For this reason the scope of the various general discographies is not identical, and any one of the early works may include items not covered by later ones. In the second place there are many sessions for which personnel details are not certain. *Jazz directory* is particularly good in such cases, being quite explicit about the nature of the problem and of the authority for any opinion given.

However, only some collectors will have access to these works: they are neither easy to buy nor commonly found in libraries. Fortunately, the publications of the 'sixties have brought us within sight of a comprehensive listing of jazz recordings from the earliest days. Brian Rust's two volumes of *Jazz records A-Z* cover the period before 1942 and are complemented by Dixon and Godrich's *Blues & gospel records 1902-1942*. The period since 1943 has been dealt with by Jorgen Grunnet Jepsen. His first four volumes published, M-Z, covered 1942-1962, the more recent volumes, A-E, are extended to 1965 and the latest comes up to 1967. The complete set should be available very soon. What is needed now are annual volumes like Albert McCarthy's *Jazz discography 1958. Jazz catalogue,* by G Cherrington and others, is a partial answer but only covers records issued in Great Britain. A new discography by Walter Bruyninchx began publication in 1968. It is in looseleaf form with an additions and amendments service.

There are three main requirements of discography: identification of all recordings made; provision of details; and listing of all issues. The first requirement is now reasonably well met by the works described above. Errors and omissions should be corrected in time. The fundamental details are also given and one cannot ask more of a general discography. In a special discography it is feasible to provide more detail. There are three outstanding works that include a great deal of information on the activities of the musicians concerned—*King Joe Oliver,* by Walter Allen and Brian Rust, *Jack Teagarden's music,* by Howard Waters, and *B.G.—off the record* by Donald Connor. Another useful item is a list of soloists for each performance, though few discographies have provided it. Those which have include *King Joe Oliver,* the selective discography in *Duke Ellington,* edited by Peter Gammond, and the Ellington discographies by Aasland (1954) and Massagli (1966).

There are, of course, other advantages to the special discography. The concentration of attention makes the sifting of fine detail possible, with the likely consequence of correcting any errors and omissions in the general discographies. There is also the great value and convenience of seeing in one sequence all the recordings of a given musician. In a general discography they are likely to be widely distributed under different headings. At the moment they cannot even be easily located, since no index has yet been published for the Jepsen volumes.

The last requirement of discography, listing all issues, is the most difficult to meet and gives rise to the biggest deficiency in currently available works. The Rust and Dixon and Godrich volumes, for example, do not attempt to list anything other than 78rpm issues. Once again, individual discographies may provide more information, but they do not between them cover the whole recorded output. Another important source of information are national discographies. The English *Jazz catalogue* has already been mentioned. Other examples are Horst Lange's *Deutsche 78er discographie.* Some national discographies are limited to recordings *made* in the country concerned, such as Giuseppe Barazetta's *Jazz inciso in Italia,* and Robert Pernet's *Jazz in Little Belgium.*

It is obvious that anyone wanting full information must go to many sources. Even when all published books and pamphlets have been taken into account there will still be some errors uncorrected, some problems unsolved, and many gaps unfilled. To meet these needs a number of specialist discographical magazines have been published. The survivors to date are *Matrix, Record research* and *Blues research. Storyville* has a high proportion of discographical information, and general magazines such as *Jazz monthly* and *Jazz journal* include articles on discography, artist listings and readers' queries columns.

The arrangement of discographies calls for some comment. For individual musicians the best method is obviously chronological. For general discographies the choice is not so obvious. The Rust and Jepsen works have established a broad chronological arrangement, which is both practicable and useful. Within each time division recordings are arranged alphabetically by the name of the recording group and chronologically under each name. Both Rust volumes have an index to musicians and presumably the Jepsen work will eventually have the same. Orin Blackstone's *Index to jazz* arranged the index to musicians in one sequence with the recording names.

The advantage of this alphabetical method is that it makes for easy access to individual items. The disadvantage is that it separates closely related items. Many bands recorded under a variety of names, so that it is more useful to use a standard name to group all the recordings, with cross references from pseudonyms and variations. This method was used by Carey and McCarthy in *Jazz directory.*

The only work to use a fundamentally different arrangement is Delaunay's *Hot discography.* There the attempt was made to classify the styles and to show the development of jazz. This is a more difficult task and probably for this reason was abandoned by later discographers. However, it is not impossible to carry out, and even if Delaunay's arrangement is not perfect it certainly makes for an interesting volume. As long as there is an adequate alphabetical index to such an arrangement, individual items can be found quite quickly. The great advantage lies in having all the similar recordings together, and a work which as a whole provides a chronicle of its period. *Hot discography* may have been superseded for accuracy and quantity of detail; it remains unique for its presentation, with a fascination that is completely lacking in a characterless alphabetical order.

Information about recordings *made* must be complemented by proper identification of each record *issued*. This is particularly important in view of the deficiency already noted in the listings of all issues of a given performance. For 78rpm records the identification mark, the matrix number, was inscribed on each side. Beyond this, the label provided limited space for further details. In the earliest days, record number, tune title and performer were all that usually appeared. With the increased serious interest in jazz, many companies added personnel details and date of recording. Since the change to microgroove records, with their printed sleeves, there is no excuse for omitting any important information. Most European companies are very good in this respect, but collectors should be warned that mistakes are sometimes made. To be quite certain, the information should be checked in discographies. The best reviews of jazz records usually draw attention to such errors. Unfortunately, American companies are often less reliable in their provision of information. Such failures may at best be regarded as irresponsibility, at worst as deliberate attempts to mislead or conceal.

The discographies discussed above are all attempts to establish complete and objective lists within a given limit. A different purpose is served by annotated record guides which select and evaluate. The earliest general work of this kind, still excellent for the period it covers, is *The jazz record book,* by Charles Edward Smith and others. The best modern examples are two editions of *Jazz on record,* published in 1960 and 1969 by Hutchinson and Hanover Books respectively. They should really be regarded as independent works, since they have only one contributor in common and the entries for the second edition are completely new. Useful for comparison and for coverage of American issues are Frederic Ramsey's *A guide to long play jazz records* and John S Wilson's *The collector's jazz: traditional and swing,* and *The collector's jazz: modern and progressive.* Harris and Rust's *Recorded jazz: a critical guide* is marred by its authors' extremely narrow view of what constitutes jazz.

Some useful contributions to this group of literature have been made by record companies. In 1939 RCA commissioned Hugues Panassié to compile *144 hot jazz records*. The English Decca company later produced *Jazz on 78s* and *Jazz on LPs*. The major English companies also produced a number of straightforward discographies in the 'forties, and Decca issued a particularly attractive discography of the London ' Origins of jazz ' series. Some useful booklets, with discographical details, have also been issued with sets of records such as the American Columbia 'Archive ' series.

THE PRINCIPAL DISCOGRAPHIES
*General*
Schleman, Hilton R: *Rhythm on record*. London, Melody Maker, 1936.

Delaunay, Charles: *Hot discographie*. Paris, Hot Jazz, 1936. Revised edition 1938.

Delaunay Charles: *Hot discography*. New York, Commodore Music Shop, 1940 (based on 1938 edition). Corrected reprint by Commodore Record Co, 1943.

Delaunay Charles: *Hot discographie 1943*. Paris, Collection du Hot Club de France, 1944.

Delaunay, Charles: *New hot discography*, edited by Walter E Schaap and George Avakian. New York, Criterion, 1948.

Delaunay, Charles: *Hot discographie encyclopédique*. Paris, Editions Jazz Disques, three volumes A-He, 1951-2.

Blackstone, Orin: *Index to jazz*. Fairfax, Va, The Record Changer, four volumes 1945-8. Second edition, Part 1 A-E, 1949.

Carey, Dave and McCarthy, Albert: *The directory of recorded jazz and swing music* (cover title: *Jazz directory*). Volumes 1-4: Fordingbridge (Hants), Delphic Press, 1949-52; volumes 2-4, second edition: London, Cassell, 1955-7; volumes 5-6: London, Cassell, 1955-7.

McCarthy, Albert: *Jazz discography 1958.* London, Cassell, 1960.

Rust, Brian: *Jazz records A-Z, 1897-1931*. Hatch End, Middlesex, The Author, 1961. Second edition 1962. Separate index by Richard Grandorge, 1963.

Rust, Brian: *Jazz records A-Z, 1932-1942*. Hatch End, Middlesex, The Author, 1965.

Dixon, Robert M W and Godrich, John: *Blues and gospel records 1902-1942*. Hatch End, Middlesex, Brian Rust, 1963.

Jepsen, Jorgen Grunnet: *Jazz Records 1942-1962*. Volumes 5-6 M-R. Copenhagen, Nordisk Tidsskrift Forlag, 1963; volumes 7-8 S-Z: Holte, Denmark, Knudsen, 1964-5.

Jepsen, Jorgen Grunnet: *Jazz records 1942-1965*. Volumes 1-3 A-El: Holte, Denmark, Knudsen, 1966-7.

Jepsen, Jorgen Grunnet: Jazz records 1942-1967. Volume 4a Ell-Goo: Holte, Denmark, Knudsen, 1968 (to be completed).

*National* (examples)

a) Records issued in one country

*England:* Discography of previous year's issues contained in 4 volumes of *Just jazz*. Peter Davies 1957, 1958; Four Square Books 1959; Souvenir Press 1960.

Cherrington, George *et al*: *Jazz catalogue*. London, Jazz Journal, 1960- (annual).

*Germany:* Lange, Horst: *Die Deutsche 78er discographie der jazz—und—hot—dance—musik 1903-1958*. Berlin, Colloquium Verlag, 1966.

b) Records made in one country

*Australia:* Mitchell, Jack: *Australian discography*. Lithgow, NSW, The Author, second edition 1960.

*Belgium:* Pernet, Robert: *Jazz in Little Belgium*. Brussels, The Author, 1966.

*Germany:* Lange, Horst: *Die geschichte des jazz in Deutschland*, Lubbecke, Verlag Uhle und Kleimann, 1960.

*Italy:* Barazetta, Giuseppe: *Jazz inciso in Italia*. Milan, Messaggerie Musicali, 1960.

*Individual*

a) Outstanding bio-discographies

Allen, Walter C and Rust, Brian: *King Joe Oliver*. Belleville, NJ, Walter C Allen, 1955 (London, Sidgwick & Jackson, 1958).

Connor, Donald Russell: *B.G.—off the record: a bio/discography of Benny Goodman*. Fairless Hills, Penn, Gaildonna Publishers, 1958.

Waters, Howard J: *Jack Teagarden's Music: his career and recordings*. Stanhope, NJ, Walter C Allen, 1960.

b) Others (examples)

Jepsen, Jorgen Grunnet: Series published in Denmark by

Debut Records, late 'fifties, including Armstrong, Ellington, Morton, Basie, Kenton, Parker, Davies, Young, Holiday, etc.

Jazz Discographies Unlimited, California: Series begun in 1965 dealing especially with big bands. See reviews in *Jazz monthly*, 1965 onwards.

Chilton, John: *Bill Coleman on record*. London, The Author, 1966.

Fairchild, Rolph: *Discography of Art Hodes*. Ontario, California, The Author, 1962.

Massagli, Luciano *et al*: *Duke Ellington's story on record*. Milan, Musica Jazz, 1966-. Several volumes in progress.

*Jazz studies* volume 2, no 3, includes a list of some 150 individual discographies published since 1960.

*Annotated record guides*

a) General

Smith, C E *et al*: *The jazz record book*. New York, Smith & Durrell, 1942.

Panassié, Hugues: *Discographie critique des meilleurs disques de jazz*. Geneva, Grasset, 1948.

Ramsey, Frederic: *A guide to longplay jazz records*. New York, Long Player Publications, 1954.

Wilson, John S: *The collectors' jazz: traditional and swing*. Philadelphia, Lippincott, 1958.

Wilson, John S: *The collectors' jazz: modern and progressive*. Philadelphia, Lippincott, 1959.

Fox, Charles *et al*: *Jazz on record: a critical guide*. London, Hutchinson, 1960.

McCarthy, Albert *et al*: *Jazz on record: a critical guide to the first 50 years: 1917-1967*. London, Hanover Books, 1968.

b) Company

Panassié, Hugues: *Hugues Panassié discusses 144 hot jazz Bluebird and Victor records*. Camden, NJ, RCA, 1939.

Decca Record Company: *Jazz on 78s*. London, 1954.

Decca Record Company: *Jazz on LPs*. London, revised edition 1956.


THE JAZZ BOOK COLLECTOR

As a subject for specialization in book collecting, jazz is as good as any other. As good, that is to say, from the point of view of interest and range of material. There are no really valuable items or examples of beautiful book-making. A comprehensive collection is not an impossible aim, though its cost would be sufficiently high to deter most people. Since subject specialization implies an interest in the subject, jazz book collecting will inevitably be subsidiary to record collecting. The basic collection will consist of books with permanent or current validity, its object to provide accurate information and perceptive evaluation, both directly enhancing the enjoyment and understanding of the music. The fundamental requirement, as we have seen, is discography. After this come other kinds of reference material and historical, biographical and critical studies. Such a collection need not be large if carefully selected, and for many, a small representative collection will be the aim. The compleat collector will not be satisfied with this utilitarian aim. For him every piece of paper connected with the subject will be of interest as part of the story of jazz, its study, acceptance and appreciation.

A happy hunting ground for such a collector is the literature published before 1940. Much of it came from Europe and was never translated into English. It has the double appeal of rarity and mystery. I have never seen an analysis of the European writing of this period, and I imagine that there are very few people in England or America who have seen more than a fraction of the items concerned. If there were any good books written in the 'twenties they are in this group. In fact, there is not a single one in English that could properly be classified as a jazz book, whatever the title implied. The best known are H O Osgood's *So this is jazz* and R W S Mendl's *The appeal of jazz*. Both authors confuse jazz with the popular music of the time; neither gives any indication that he had ever heard a real jazz musician. Despite good intentions they probably did more harm than good. The influence is still to be seen in the incredibly misinformed entry for jazz in the current edition of the *Oxford companion to music*.

If the keyword for the 'twenties is ignorance, that for the 'thirties is enthusiasm; and the two names most closely associated with this characteristic are Robert Goffin and Hugues Panassié. Although Goffin was the earlier writer he was not translated into English until 1944. Panassié's *Hot jazz* was translated in 1936, thus achieving the distinction of being the first serious analysis of the musical form to appear in English. It succeeded, where Osgood and Mendl had failed ten years before, in explaining the essence of the music and introducing the leading musicians. In the light of today's knowledge it is easy enough to find faults with the book, but such criticism is inappropriate. For its time and place it was remarkably well informed and perceptive. I doubt if any other book has been so effective in arousing enthusiasm for the music. If the spirit rather than the letter is accepted as the prime factor in this function, I can think of many worse introductions to the subject even today.

BIBLIOGRAPHIES

The first attempt at a jazz bibliography was made by H Meunier Harris, in *The jazzfinder '49*. He listed some 90 books, 90 pamphlets and 80 periodicals. Alan Merriam's *A bibliography of jazz* was published five years later but set its limit at the end of 1950. In the introduction, the author says that the list is neither selective nor complete. I think we can take that to imply the inclusion of every book, pamphlet and periodical (113 listed) known to him. In all there are well over 3,000 items, but most of them are articles from newspapers, magazines and essay collections. Nearly 300 periodicals, general and special, are represented, but unfortunately there is no indication how thoroughly each was indexed. Why, for example, are there entries for only one issue of the American journal *Playback*? My other complaint is that the subject index is far too broad. One may be forced to look up a hundred entries or more to find one or two that are relevant. Despite the criticisms, this is a useful work and the fullest bibliography published to date.

The second edition of R G Reisner's *The literature of jazz* was published in 1959. This is described as a selective bibliography and includes some items published as late as 1959. The list of books and pamphlets is very full and there are some thousand articles drawn from periodicals not specializing in jazz. The most recent, but much more selective, list of books is the *Readers' guide to books on jazz* by J R Haselgrove and D Kennington. *Jazz catalogue*, already mentioned in the discography section, has been published annually since 1960. Each issue includes a list of books and an index of periodical articles.

Between them these publications obviously cover a good proportion of the books and pamphlets that have been published, but we still await the definitive retrospective bibliography. Periodical articles present a far more formidable problem and a comprehensive index to jazz magazines before 1960 seems a forlorn hope.

One project that is feasible and highly desirable is a good critical bibliography. There is a great deal of rubbish amongst the literature of jazz and many books with faults and limitations. The most perceptive annotated list that I have seen is in William Austin's *Music in the 20th century*, 1966. It includes about fifty books and twenty articles. Alan Merriam compiled a short bibliography for the *Music Library Association notes* in 1953. It includes 163 items with annotations but the observations are not so acute as Austin's. For criticism of the full range of jazz books the student must refer to reviews in periodicals. In my opinion the best single source is *Jazz monthly*.

### ENCYCLOPEDIAS AND OTHER REFERENCE BOOKS

The distinction between reference books and books meant for consecutive reading is not absolute, but the content and/or arrangement puts some quite definitely in the reference category. Discographies and bibliographies are clear cut examples, and so are books consisting of short entries arranged in alphabetical order of their subject. These may be called encyclopedias, dictionaries, guides or indexes. Dictionaries, in the precise sense, have more social than musical significance in jazz. In other alphabetically arranged works details of musicians occupy most space. The best known are those by Leonard Feather and Hugues Panassié, which are complementary rather than competitive. More specialized is the recently published *New Orleans jazz: a family album*, by Al Rose and Edmond Souchon, which is a profusely illustrated guide to the musicians, bands and places of New Orleans. Even more limited in scope is Samuel Charters' *Jazz: New Orleans 1885-1963*, which deals only with negro musicians who played in the city.

George Simon's *The big bands* is a comprehensive guide to the swing bands. Stanley Dance's *Jazz era: the 'forties* is the only one yet to appear of a projected four volume series. It gives brief biographical and critical details for each musician and a selected list of his recordings during the period.

Guides to popular music usually include some relevant information, including details of themes used for jazz improvisation and their composers. There are also several indexes to American popular songs.

Pleasure in pictorial information is not limited to children of the McLuhan age. Understanding and appreciation in any field of endeavour would be considerably impoverished without such aid. Many jazz books include illustrations, a few are mainly pictorial. Of these, Rose and Souchon's *New Orleans jazz: a family album* is the finest for quantity, quality and rarity. Other examples are Keepnews and Grauer's *A pictorial history of jazz*, Rosenkrantz's *Swing photo album*, and Stock and Hentoff's *Jazz street*. The latest, *Preservation Hall portraits*, is unique in containing reproductions of paintings rather than photographs. The artist, Noel Rockmore, has succeeded in conveying very powerfully the spirit of many New Orleans musicians. A jazz calendar, with photographs of musicians, has been produced for the last ten years by Joachim Berendt. Wider in scope, but of great interest to jazz, is *Black magic: a pictorial history of the negro in American entertainment*, by Langston Hughes and Milton Meltzer.

Handbooks form an indeterminate category of books which may be regarded as primarily for reference. Barry Ulanov's *A handbook of jazz* deals with various aspects of the subject, but in no great detail. According to the dust jacket it was written for ' the interested general reader '. The index of musicians, with 600 names, claims to be ' as comprehensive as possible '. Rose and Souchon's *New Orleans jazz: a family album* lists 1,000 musicians from New Orleans alone!

## THE PRINCIPAL REFERENCE BOOKS
### Bibliographies

Merriam, A P: *A bibliography of jazz*. Philadelphia, American Folklore Society, 1954.

Reisner, R G: *The literature of jazz: a selective bibliography*. New York Public Library, 1959.

Haselgrove, J R & Kennington, D: *Readers' guide to books on jazz*. London, Library Association, County Libraries Group, second edition, 1965.

Cherrington, G *et al*: *Jazz catalogue*. London, Jazz Journal, 1960-.

*Encyclopedias and biographical dictionaries*
a) General
Feather, Leonard: *The encyclopedia of jazz.* New York, Horizon Press, 1955 (London, Barker, 1956).
Feather, Leonard: *The encyclopedia yearbook of jazz.* New York, Horizon Press, 1956 (London, Barker, 1957).
Feather, Leonard: *The new yearbook of jazz.* New York, Horizon Press, 1958 (London, Barker, 1959).
Feather, Leonard: *Encyclopedia of jazz in the sixties.* New York, Horizon Press, 1966.
Panassié, Hugues & Gautier, Madeleine: *Dictionary of jazz.* London, Cassell, 1956.
b) Special aspects
Charters, Samuel: *Jazz: New Orleans 1885-1963. An index to the negro musicians of New Orleans.* New York, Oak Publications, revised edition, 1963.
Rose, Al & Souchon, Edmond: *New Orleans jazz: a family album.* Baton Rouge, Louisiana State University Press, 1967.
Dance, Stanley (ed): *Jazz era: the 'forties.* London, MacGibbon & Kee, 1961.
Simon, George T: *The big bands.* New York, Macmillan, 1967.
*Iconography*
Hughes, Langston & Meltzer, Milton: *Black magic: a pictorial history of the negro in American entertainment.* Englewood Cliffs, NJ, Prentice-Hall, 1967.
Keepnews, Orrin & Grauer, Bill: *A pictorial history of jazz.* New York, Crown Publishers, second edition 1966.
Rockmore, Noel: *Preservation Hall portraits.* Baton Rouge, Louisiana State University Press, 1968. (Text by Larry Borenstein and Bill Russell.)
Rosencrantz, Timme: *Swing photo album 1939.* Lowestoft, Scorpion Press, second edition 1964.
Rose, Al & Souchon, Edmond: *New Orleans jazz: a family album.* Baton Rouge, Louisiana State University Press, 1967.
Stock, Dennis and Hentoff, Nat: *Jazz street.* New York, Doubleday, 1960 (London, Deutsch, 1960).
*Popular music*
Burton, Jack: *The blue book of Broadway musicals.* 1952.
Burton, Jack: *The blue book of Hollywood musicals.* 1953.

Burton, Jack: *The blue book of Tin Pan Alley.* 1951. (New edition in two volumes 1962-65.)

Burton, Jack: *The index of American popular music.* 1957. (All four titles published by Century House, Watkins Glen, New York.)

Gammond, Peter and Clayton, Peter: *A guide to popular music.* London, Phoenix House, 1960.

Mattfield, Julius. *Variety music cavalcade 1620-1961: a chronology of vocal and instrumental music popular in the United States.* Englewood Cliffs, NJ, Prentice-Hall, revised edition 1962.

Shapiro, Nat: *Popular music: an annotated index of American popular songs.* New York, Adrian Press. Five volumes in progress. Volume I 1950-1959, 1964; volume II 1940-1949, 1965; volume III 1960-1969, 1967; volume IV 1930-1939, 1968.

Spaeth, Sigmund: *A history of popular music in America.* New York, Random House, 1948 (London, Phoenix House, 1960).

Stambler, Irwin: *Encyclopaedia of popular music.* New York, St Martin's Press, 1965.

## THE CATEGORIES OF JAZZ WRITING

Apart from reference books, the main categories of jazz writing are: history; biography; autobiography; social analysis; musical analysis; criticism of individual musicians and performances; technical guides—how to compose, arrange and play. Periodical articles and pamphlets usually represent pure examples of these categories. Except for the technical publications, books are usually mixed. For example, introductions and general surveys may be comprehensive; histories usually include social and musical analysis and sometimes biography and criticism; books on individual musicians are nearly always a mixture of biography and criticism and may include discography as well. In a system for organizing literature both pure and mixed categories must be taken into account. This problem will be discussed in chapter 3. The following broad classification is used as a convenience for grouping books according to their main emphasis. As the technical books are for musicians rather than collectors I have merely listed some examples at the end of the chapter.

## INTRODUCTIONS AND GENERAL SURVEYS

At the beginning of the 'sixties there was a sudden spate of primers with such titles as *Know about jazz, Enjoy jazz* and *I like jazz.*

Most of them are all right as introductions for children or general readers, though *Teach yourself jazz,* by Martin Lindsay, is hardly the best book one would choose for the purpose. These elementary works can be ignored by intending collectors. The one exception I would make is Charles Fox's *Jazz in perspective,* which is the best concise summary of jazz history—and beautifully illustrated. Martin Williams' *Where's the melody?,* although described as a listener's introduction to jazz, is really a collection of essays, not all of which are elementary.

There are only two general surveys at a more advanced level. Francis Newton's *The jazz scene,* is the more comprehensive and, in my opinion, the better work. Leonard Feather's *The book of jazz* is particularly valuable for its chapter called ' The anatomy of improvisation '. A record containing the analysed solos was issued by Verve (MGV 8230) and English Columbia (33CX 10141).

COMPOSITE WORKS : ESSAYS, YEARBOOKS AND PERIODICALS
Essay collections usually attempt to preserve the more important writings that have appeared in periodicals. Sometimes the contributions do not deserve such honour. Most of *The jazz word,* edited by Dom Cerulli, falls into this class. Two of the best collections are those edited by Martin Williams: *The art of jazz* and *Jazz panorama.* For one person's lively and perceptive response to jazz performances and recordings year by year, the three volumes by Whitney Balliett are unique. Very few negro writers have so far contributed to jazz literature, but Ralph Ellison has several fine essays in *Shadow and act.*

Yearbooks are usually a mixture of items referring to the past year's activities, which may have permanent reference value, and others which might have appeared in any periodical. The only one extant is *Downbeat's,* its competitor *Metronome* having ceased publication in the early 'sixties. Other yearbooks lasted only a short while: *Esquire* 1944-47, *Poetry London* 1946-47, *Jazzfinder* 1949, *Jazzways* 1949, and *Just Jazz* 1957-60. They all contain some worthwhile material, though the *Esquire* volumes would have been better for less of their editor's writing.

Jazz periodicals fall into three broad categories: discographical, collectors ', and general. The discographical have already been mentioned. Collectors' magazines often begin as vehicles for the sale or exchange of records. The most famous was the American

*Record changer,* which quickly expanded to include articles and reviews devoted to early jazz. The tradition continues today in the American *Jazz report* and the English *Storyville.* The English *Vintage jazz mart* and *RSVP* consist mainly of lists of records for sale and exchange.

General periodicals have been published in most countries of the world, but their life is usually brief. The two main English periodicals, *Jazz journal* and *Jazz monthly,* are among the few exceptions. *Jazz monthly* produces the higher proportion of articles with permanent value, and the highest quality reviews of records and books. *Jazz journal* contains more items of news and a greater variety of material. Both are worth buying.

Periodicals devoted to popular as well as jazz music find it easier to make a living. *The melody maker* has had a long life in England, though its jazz content is now rather small. The American *Jazz* changed its title recently to *Jazz and pop, Metronome* and *Downbeat* both moved away from popular music. *Metronome* ceased publication when its quality was highest. *Downbeat* continues.

## HISTORY AND SOCIAL ANALYSIS

History consists not only of facts but also of their interpretation. We may therefore distinguish between primary sources supplying evidence and secondary works in which the evidence is selected and interpreted. The first category would include musicians' reminiscences. In *Hear me talkin' to ya,* Hentoff and Shapiro arranged an anthology of quotations from 200 musicians to form an historical sequence.

Some of this evidence for jazz history is not in written form and I have already referred to the oral history project at Tulane University. A few items have been issued on commercial labels including the Folkways ' Music of New Orleans ', compiled by Samuel Charters (FA 2461/5); ' The legend of Willie " The Lion " Smith ' (Top Rank RX 3015); ' Coleman Hawkins: a documentary ' (Riverside RLP 117/8); and Lil Armstrong's ' Satchmo and me ' (Riverside RLP 120). The most famous of these recordings, by Jelly Roll Morton, has not been available for some time. Though it is no substitute for the musical examples, Alan Lomax's *Mr Jelly Roll* does contain Morton's commentary. The statements of these musicians must be seen in the light of their own characters and in relation to all other evidence available. Perry Bradford's *Born with the blues*, for example, has a good deal of information about the early days in New York, but many of its claims and judgments are not to be taken seriously.

Chronicles, which merely relate a series of events, also belong to this category of primary sources. Actual examples will not necessarily be 'pure', but a book such as *Jazz: a history of the New York scene*, by Charters and Kunstadt, will be more fairly judged if it is classed as a chronicle.

Jazz histories may be comprehensive, attempting to recount the most significant facts and to explain the main developments in the music; or they may be specialized, providing more detail about one period or aspect. There can never be a definitive general history of anything, since time always changes our perspective. It may also bring to light hitherto unknown facts. Martin Williams' essay 'Last trip up the river' in *Where's the melody?* is one indication that we are due for a new interpretation of jazz history. The collection entitled *Jazz: new perspectives on the history* . . . contains a good deal of information not accounted for in previous works. Within the limitations of its time Marshall Stearns' *The story of jazz* is the best of the jazz histories. Earlier books, such as Ramsey and Smith's *Jazzmen,* Wilder Hobson's *American jazz music,* and Iain Lang's *Jazz in perspective,* are still readable for details and individual judgments. The most useful volumes for the modern period are *Modern jazz: developments since 1939,* by Horricks and Morgan, and *The jazz cataclysm,* by Barry McRae.

To deepen his knowledge and understanding of the origins of jazz the collector must turn to general works on Afro-American music, such as H Courlander's *Negro folk music, USA;* to the history of ragtime, fully documented by Blesh and Janis in *They all played ragtime,* and to studies of the blues.

The histories of jazz inevitably refer to social factors, but it is only recently that books concerned primarily with social analysis have begun to appear. Francis Newton's was the first to give it prominence, in *The jazz scene.* In the 'sixties we have had *The jazz life,* by Nat Hentoff, *Jazz and the white Americans,* by Neil Leonard, *Blues people,* by Le Roi Jones, and *Four lives in the bebop business,* by A B Spellman.

64

Books in this category may be roughly divided into three groups: those concerned solely with the elements of jazz (melody, rhythm, harmony etc); those which include a general analysis of the main styles, musicians and bands; and those which include detailed analysis of particular performances.

A clear and simple introduction to the elements was published in 1968 by Avril Dankworth, with the title *Jazz: an introduction to its musical basis*. The only previous work devoted entirely to the elements was the more detailed *Jazz: hot and hybrid*, by Winthrop Sargeant; its latest edition has the misleading title *Jazz: a history*.

The earliest book of the second kind to be published in English was Panassié's *Hot jazz*. A sound, recent book in similar form is Joachim Berendt's *The new jazz book*. More like the histories is Sidney Finkelstein's *Jazz: a people's music*. This is one of the books that survives well the passage of time. Its treatment of the blues and other compositions used for improvisation is particularly interesting.

The most thorough book of musical analysis is the latest— *Early jazz: its roots and musical development*, by Gunther Schuller. It makes use of the latest research in examining the African origins of jazz and includes many detailed analyses of particular performances. The work will be completed in a second volume. In his preface, Schuller refers to some of the earlier jazz writers and to the small quantity of detailed musical analysis. Surprisingly, he makes no mention of the very fine work by Leroy Ostransky, *The anatomy of jazz*. Nor does he mention the limitation of Hodeir's *Jazz: its evolution and essence*. Hodeir is a fine critic of mainstream and modern styles. His criticism of earlier jazz is worthless, since he judges it by standards appropriate only to later forms. This 'historical fallacy' is implicit in his extraordinary belief in the 'progress' of art. A complementary limitation is to be found in those writers who believe that the nature of jazz was determined for all time by its original form. Though he has since modified his views, Rudi Blesh showed this limitation in *Shining trumpets*. Despite this, the book was valuable for its emphasis on the African elements of jazz and for many analyses of performances by New Orleans musicians.

Classical musicians and musicologists were slow to discover

jazz: Ernest Ansermet's early appreciation of Sidney Bechet was an isolated phenomenon; the influence on European composers of the 'twenties was superficial. Constant Lambert, in *Music ho!*, showed that he had listened to real jazz but had failed to understand its essence. Only since the last war do we find the development of real understanding. Gunther Schuller, Leroy Ostransky and the more famous Leonard Bernstein are examples of American classical musicians who have taken a serious interest in jazz. It was left to an English musicologist, however, to produce the best study of jazz in its setting. *Music in a new found land,* by Wilfrid Mellers, not only analyses jazz in detail but also shows its relationships with the folk, popular and art forms of American music.

INDIVIDUAL MUSICIANS: AUTOBIOGRAPHY, BIOGRAPHY AND CRITICISM

The centre of jazz interest is the individual musician. Fittingly enough, the first autobiography was Louis Armstrong's *Swing that music,* published in 1936. Since that time many other musicians have told their own stories, often with the help of ghost writers who don't usually improve the quality of the literature. Despite this, most of them have some interest. Notable examples are Sidney Bechet's *Treat it gentle,* Mezzrow's *Really the blues,* and Billie Holiday's *Lady sings the blues.* The quality of these books is not necessarily related to the musical status of the authors. Artie Shaw's *The trouble with Cinderella* is one of the most interesting and well written; Benny Goodman, a more important musician, contributed one of the worst in *The kingdom of swing.*

Monographs on individual musicians are usually a mixture of biography and criticism. Cassell produced a useful series in the *Kings of jazz* between 1959 and 1963, which were only disappointing in the rather limited discographies they included. A comparable American series is Macmillan's *Jazz masters,* each volume dealing with the most important musicians of one decade. Other good books devoting chapters to selected musicians are *The jazz makers,* edited by Hentoff and Shapiro, *These jazzmen of our time,* edited by Raymond Horricks, *Essays on jazz,* by Burnett James, and *The reluctant art,* by Benny Green.

The two most important bands in the history of jazz have been well treated in *Count Basie and his orchestra,* by Raymond

Horricks, and *Duke Ellington: his life and music,* edited by Peter Gammond.

## BAD BOOKS AND FLAWED BOOKS

The newcomer to jazz may realize that the earliest literature is liable to be misleading or inadequate. He is less likely to be aware of limitations in the more recent writings. Ignorance of real jazz in writings of the 'twenties is not surprising; contemporary ignorance *is*, particularly when sponsored by a reputable publishing house such as English Universities Press in their ' Teach yourself' series. There was no excuse for leaving the volume on jazz to someone who is not an accepted authority. Unfortunately, this cavalier attitude to jazz is not uncommon and one must be particularly careful of general books on music.

Less blameworthy than ignorance, but certainly to be avoided, is bad writing. Dave Dexter's *The jazz story,* for example, is execrable in style, superficial in facts and judgments. *The jazz word,* edited by Dom Cerulli, often displays the worst excesses of jazz writing. Stephen Longstreet's purple passages in *Sportin' House* are equally objectionable; particularly since the book has little to do with jazz, perpetuating as it does the perversely ' romantic ' belief in its close connection with New Orleans brothels. Longstreet's book is an aspect of the sentimentality to which American writers on jazz are particularly prone. Studs Terkel's *Giants of jazz* is a collection of grossly sentimental fantasies. Wareing and Garlick, in *Bugles for Beiderbecke,* may have avoided the fantasy, but not the sentimentality.

The last fault about which warning must be given is that of partisan writing. Books in this category are not to be dismissed. They are often extremely good on their chosen ground, but not to be trusted outside it. I have already cited as examples André Hodeir's *Jazz: its evolution and essence* and Rudi Blesh's *Shining trumpets.* Grossman and Farrell's *The heart of jazz* follows the same line as *Shining trumpets,* but is not in the same class for scholarship or perception. It is further disfigured by its special pleading for the religious nature of early jazz. A more specialized example of partisanship is H O Brunn's *The story of the Original Dixieland Jazz Band.* This is valuable for its factual details, but completely misleading as to the significance of the ODJB.

67

Most of these books have appeared in a variety of forms on both sides of the Atlantic. The following list gives only the latest editions in the country of origin. For American books the latest (or paperback) English issue is also given.

*Introduction and general surveys*

Feather, Leonard: *The book of jazz from then till now.* New York, Horizon, 1965.

Fox, Charles: *Jazz in perspective.* London, BBC, 1969.

Newton, Francis: *The jazz scene.* London, MacGibbon & Kee, 1959 (Penguin, 1961).

*Essays*

Balliett, Whitney: *The sound of surprise.* New York, Dutton, 1959 (London, Penguin, 1963).

Balliett, Whitney: *Dinosaurs in the morning.* Philadelphia, Lippincott, 1962 (London, Jazz Book Club, 1965).

Balliett, Whitney: *Such sweet thunder.* Indianapolis, Bobbs-Merrill, 1966 (London, Macdonald, 1968).

Ellison, Ralph: *Shadow and act.* New York, Random House, 1964 (London, Secker & Warburg, 1967).

Williams, Martin (*ed*): *The art of jazz.* New York, Oxford University Press, 1959 (London, Jazz Book Club, 1962).

Williams, Martin (*ed*): *Jazz panorama.* New York, Crowell-Collier, 1962 (London, Jazz Book Club, 1965).

Williams, Martin: *Where's the melody?* New York, Pantheon, 1966.

*History and origins*

Blesh, R and Janis, H: *They all played ragtime.* New York, Grove Press, revised edition 1959 (London, Sidgwick & Jackson, 1958).

Courlander, H: *Negro folk music, USA.* Columbia University Press, 1963 (London, Jazz Book Club, 1966).

Hentoff, N & McCarthy, A (*eds*): *Jazz: new perspectives in the history of jazz.* New York, Rinehart, 1959 (London, Jazz Book Club, 1962).

Hentoff, N & Shapiro, N (*eds*): *Hear me talking to ya.* New York, Rinehart, 1955 (London, Penguin, 1962).

Horricks, R & Morgan, A: *Modern jazz: developments since 1939.* London, Gollancz, 1956.

McRae, Barry: *The jazz cataclysm*. London, Dent, 1967.

Oliver, Paul: *Blues fell this morning*. London, Cassell, 1960.

Oliver, Paul: *Conversation with the blues*. London, Cassell, 1965.

Oliver, Paul: *Screening the blues*. London, Cassell, 1968.

Oliver, Paul: *The story of the blues*. London, Barrie and Rockliff, 1969.

Stearns, Marshall: *The story of jazz*. New York, Oxford University Press, 1956 (London, Muller, 1958).

*Social analysis*

Hentoff, N: *The jazz life*. New York, Dial Press, 1961 (London, Hamilton, 1964).

Jones, LeRoi: *Blues people*. New York, Morrow, 1963 (London, Jazz Book Club, 1966).

Leonard, Neil: *Jazz and the white Americans: the acceptance of a new art form*. Chicago University Press, 1962 (London, Jazz Book Club, 1964).

Spellman, A B: *Four lives in the bebop business*. New York, Pantheon, 1966 (London, MacGibbon & Kee, 1967).

*Musical analysis*

Berendt, J: *The new jazz book*. New York, Hill & Wang, 1962 (London, Jazz Book Club, 1965).

Blesh, R: *Shining trumpets*. New York, Knopf, second edition 1958 (London, Cassell, 1958).

Dankworth, Avril: *Jazz: an introduction to its musical basis*. (London, Oxford University Press, 1968).

Finkelstein, S: *Jazz: a people's music*. New York, Citadel, 1948 (London, Jazz Book Club, 1964).

Hodeir, André: *Jazz: its evolution and essence*. London, Secker & Warburg, 1956.

Mellers, Wilfrid: *Music in a new found land*. London, Barrie & Rockliff, 1964.

Ostransky, Leroy: *The anatomy of jazz*. Seattle, University of Washington Press, 1960.

Sargeant, Winthrop: *Jazz: a history*. New York, McGraw Hill, second edition 1964.

Schuller, Gunther: *Early jazz: its roots and musical development*. London & New York, Oxford University Press, 1968.

## Musicians: autobiography

Armstrong, Louis: *Swing that music.* London, Longmans, 1936.

Armstrong, Louis: *Satchmo: my life in New Orleans.* New York, Prentice-Hall, 1954 (London, Jazz Book Club, 1957).

Bechet, Sidney: *Treat it gentle.* New York, Hill & Wang, 1960 (London, Transworld, 1964).

Holiday, Billie: *Lady sings the blues.* New York, Doubleday, 1956 (London, Barrie and Rockliff, 1958).

Lomax, Alan: *Mr Jelly Roll.* New York & London, Duell, 1950 (London, Pan, 1959).

Mezzrow, Milton: *Really the blues.* New York, Random House, 1946 (London, Transworld, 1961).

Shaw, Artie: *The trouble with Cinderella.* New York, Farrar, Straus & Young, 1952 (London, Jarrolds, 1955).

## Musicians: biography and criticism

Cassell's ' Kings of jazz series ', 1959-1963: *Louis Armstrong* by A J McCarthy; *Bix Beiderbecke* by Burnett James; *Miles Davis* by Michael James; *Johnny Dodds* by G E Lambert; *Duke Ellington* by G E Lambert; *Dizzy Gillespie* by Michael James; *Coleman Hawkins* by A J McCarthy; *Jellyroll Morton* by Martin Williams; *King Oliver* by Martin Williams; *Charlie Parker* by Max Harrison; *Bessie Smith* by Paul Oliver; *Fats Waller* by Charles Fox.

Gammond, P (ed). *Duke Ellington; his life and music.* London, Pheonix House, 1958.

Green, Benny: *The reluctant art.* London, MacGibbon & Kee, 1962.

Horricks, R: *Count Basie and his orchestra.* London, Gollancz, 1957.

Horricks, R (ed): *These jazzmen of our time.* London, Gollancz, 1959.

James, Burnett: *Essays on jazz.* London, Sidgwick & Jackson, 1961.

Macmillan's ' Jazz masters ' series: *Jazz masters of the 'twenties* by Richard Hadlock, 1966. *Jazz masters of the 'forties* by Ira Gitler, 1966. *Jazz masters of the 'fifties* by Joe Goldberg, 1965. *Jazz masters of New Orleans* by Martin Williams 1967. *Jazz masters of the swing era* (in preparation).

Shapiro, N and Hentoff, N (eds): *The jazzmakers.* New York, Rinehart, 1957 (London, Peter Davies, 1958).

70

*Institutions and media*

Allen, Richard B: 'New Orleans Jazz Archive at Tulane'. *Wilson library bulletin* (USA), March 1966, pp 619-623.

Balliett, W: 'Trove'. Pp. 144-154 in *Dinosaurs in the morning*. Phoenix, 1962. (On jazz films.)

'Chicago Jazz Society off to flying start'. *Downbeat* (USA), May 1 1969, pp. 13-14.

Hall, David: 'The collectors organize'. *Hi fi/stereo review* (USA), March 1967, pp 44, 46.

Harris, Sheldon: 'The Institute of Jazz studies'. *Jazz journal*, June 1963, pp 23-24.

'International Association of Jazz Record Collectors'. *Storyville* 21, February/March 1968, pp 104-5.

Langridge, D W: 'Jazz and libraries'. *The library world*, March 1966, p 260.

Morgenstern, Dan: 'Jazz on film'. *Downbeat music '67* (12th yearbook) (USA), pp 64-68, 86-91.

New Orleans Jazz Club: *New Orleans Jazz Museum: 5th anniversary celebration*. 1966.

Newton, Francis: 'Jazz concerts'. Pp 11-16 in Williamson, Ken (*ed*): *This is jazz*. Newnes, 1960.

Whannel, R: *Jazz on film*. British Film Institute, 1966.

Witherden, B A: 'British Institute of Jazz studies'. *Jazz monthly*, February 1969, p 31.

*Discography and record history*

Black, Douglas C: 'Matrix numbers—their meaning and history'. Melbourne, *Australian jazz quarterly*, 1946.

Blackstone, Orin: 'Modern record research'. Pp 143-150 in *The jazzfinder '49*. New Orleans, Blackstone, 1949.

Graham, Charles: 'Jazz and the phonograph'. Pp 155-166 in Feather, L: *The new yearbook of jazz*. Barker, 1959.

Hoefer, George: 'Discographies fill vital role in collectors' work'. *Downbeat* (USA), October 20 1950.

McCarthy, A J: 'Discography today'. *Jazz monthly*, October 1958, pp 26-27.

McCarthy, A J: 'Discography today'. *Jazz monthly*, February 1964, pp 2-3.

Mahony, Dan: *The Columbia 13/14000 D series*. Stanhope, NJ, Walter C Allen, second edition 1966.

Moon, Bucklin: 'Some notes on discographies'. *Record changer* (USA), November 1952, p 9.

Moon, Pete: 'Bibliography of discographies'. *Jazz studies*, volume 2 no 3, pp 44-48.

Oliver, Paul: 'The numbers game'. *Jazzbeat*, February 1966, pp 10-11.

Oliver, Paul: 'The number runners'. *Jazzbeat*, April 1966.

'Record labels in jazz history'. Pp 107-128 in *The jazzfinder '49*. New Orleans, Blackstone, 1949.

Sheatsley, Paul B: 'A quarter century of jazz discography'. *Record research*, no 58 (USA), February 1964, pp 3-6.

Venables, R G V: 'On the development of discography as an aid to jazz appreciation'. Pp 140-144 in McCarthy A (*ed*): *PL yearbook of jazz 1946*. Editions Poetry London, 1946.

Wyler, Michael: *A glimpse at the past*. Jazz Publications, 1957.

# The collection—1 classifying and indexing the literature

ARRANGEMENT OF BOOKS AND INDEXES: For all but the smallest collection, a systematic order is necessary to the useful arrangement of books. In libraries the books must be marked with symbols (notation) to preserve the order, but most private collectors will find that they can manage without this aid. In the last chapter I discussed the major categories of jazz books, from which we could construct a broad classification such as the following:

Afro-American music
  Religious—spirituals etc
  Secular—worksongs etc
    Blues
    Ragtime
    Jazz
      Reference books—bibliographies, encyclopedias, discographies
      Collections—essays, yearbooks, periodicals
      Social analysis
      History and musical analysis
      Individual musicians
    Jazz-tinged popular music

Most jazz books would find their place in this scheme, but if the subject of each were to be distinctly indicated (eg *The trumpet in jazz, The big bands, Early Jazz*), then rather more detail would be necessary as I shall show in this chapter.

The systematic order of a classification scheme is also the best method of arranging an index, since it brings together related subjects and avoids many difficulties that arise if words and phrases are used as subject headings. An alphabetical list of subjects is a necessary part of the classified index, but it serves only as a guide to the contents, not as a method of arrangement.

The long experience of libraries shows conclusively that good alphabetical subject indexes are more difficult to construct than classified indexes. Furthermore, it is wrong to think that classification plays no part in an alphabetical subject index. Consciously or unconsciously, classification must be used in choosing subject headings, in deciding on the order of terms when more than one is necessary to describe a subject, and in constructing an effective set of cross references. This is not the place to develop this argument in detail. For those who wish to pursue the subject further I have listed a few suitable books in the bibliography at the end of this chapter. To the subject of classification I shall return.

INDEXING POLICY

For standard procedures in making author and title entries and in describing documents I must refer readers once again to the general literature. I shall confine my discussion to the more difficult problem of subject indexing.

To begin with we must distinguish between indexing a whole item and indexing its contents. For example, *Jazz: a history of the New York scene*, by Charters and Kunstadt, may be summarised as ' History of jazz in New York '. In a library index (catalogue) this would appear under either a subject heading such as Jazz—History—New York, or a classification symbol such as AMT(YTF). This procedure, known as summarization, is adequate for isolating the subject of one book from the many others in a library. It does not help, however, in finding any specific item of information within the book. For example, one may wish to read about the Cotton Club, and only a detailed index of the contents of a book will serve such needs. The index to *Jazz: a history of the New York scene* contains some 1,600 items. This detailed indexing of contents is known as 'depth indexing '.

On the whole, the private collector as well as the librarian will rely on published book indexes; but he may wish to supplement them with a selective index of his own. This would be mainly for those aspects of jazz in which he had a special interest, but it could include entries for articles in collections of essays and for the major subjects in books published without an index.

For a collection of periodicals, the private index is the only satisfactory solution. Many jazz periodicals have not published their own index; general indexes, such as *Music index, Jazz cata-*

*logue* and Merriam's *Bibliography of jazz,* by no means cover all the published material. Even if one could acquire a complete set of these publications they would be unwieldy to use. A private index will be compact and refer precisely to one's own collection. It will neither contain items that are not in the collection nor lack items that are. A further advantage is its ability to show in one sequence everything on a given subject, whether in the form of a book, part of a book, periodical article, sleeve note, or programme note.

For fuller details of the techniques of subject indexing I must also refer readers to the readings at the end of this chapter. The main decisions for the private indexer are *a*) how precise he should be in describing any item and *b*) how far he should index detailed contents of items as well as their main subject. The general rule is that the more detail you put into indexing, the less time you spend in searching. This rule will obviously be interpreted in relation to the size of a collection. For a small collection, the extra time needed in searching owing to scanty indexing may be no problem; for a large collection it could be serious.

If our index contains only two items on Duke Ellington, then ' Duke Ellington ' may be sufficient description, since the time involved in checking two items is not great. Twenty items, however, could waste a lot of time if they weren't more precisely indexed as, for example, ' Duke Ellington as composer ' or ' Duke Ellington's tour of England 1963 '. It is no use relying on titles to do this detailed sorting out since they are rarely precise descriptions of an article.

The indexing of detailed contents must be entirely related to individual needs. As a general guide, priority would be claimed by the subjects of special interest to the collector, and also by those items which could not easily be predicted as part of a given article. One could predict a mention of Johnny Hodges in an article on Ellington, but not a mention of Sidney Bechet.

General libraries, then, are likely to limit themselves to their own summarization for the books, and to published indexes for the periodicals. Libraries with special collections of music may give rather more analytical entries in the catalogue for subjects of essays in collections. To provide a good service of jazz information they would have to compile their own index to periodicals rather than rely on published indexes. (Of course, before they do that they must *acquire* the periodicals. At the moment I don't know of any library in Britain that has a good jazz collection.) The private collector will usually be best served by a selective index to books, essays and periodical articles.

## CLASSIFICATION

General libraries are nearly all classified by one of the big standard schemes. In an article for *Brio*, Spring 1967, I showed that none of them has anything like adequate provision for jazz and related music. The best classification for music is the *British catalogue of music classification*, compiled by E J Coates, but even this does not treat jazz satisfactorily. In the same article I analysed its faults and suggested a possible structural change to accommodate Afro-American music as a whole. For music libraries this may be the best solution. In this chapter I shall aim at an ideal system for the jazz specialist.

Specialization does not mean that one can ignore all other subjects. Most jazz collectors will be interested in other forms of Afro-American music; some literature discusses relationships between jazz and European music, and then there are social and economic aspects of the subject. I have attempted to provide as much detail as anyone will need for classifying books and articles on jazz and other forms of Afro-American music originating in the United States. A section for other Afro-American traditions is available for development, and all other subjects are given in outline only. There are thus four main sections to the scheme, arranged in order of their relevance—Jazz; Other forms of Afro-American music; European and other traditions of music; All other subjects. Within each section I have observed the usual convention of putting the more general subject before the more special.

In jazz, as in any other field of study, there are simple subjects represented by one concept and compound subjects represented by two or more concepts. ' Improvisation ' and ' Dixieland ' are examples of the former; ' West Coast jazz in the 'twenties ' and ' The difference between early and modern negro jazz ' are examples of the latter. Since all compound subjects can be constructed from simple subjects, and since the actual combinations needed are difficult to predict, there is only one satisfactory method of constructing a classification scheme. All elementary terms must be listed and rules given for their combination. In this way any subject, however complex, will be accounted for. One further requirement is that the elementary terms should be grouped in categories. This is both desirable, as a method of effectively collecting all relevant terms, and necessary in bringing together related subjects and avoiding problems of cross-classification.

The most important category in jazz is that of the musicians themselves. The only problem is whether they should be arranged in one alphabetical sequence or further subdivided by style and function. The functions of composing, arranging, leading and performing are not as distinct in jazz as in European music, and many musicians play more than one instrument. It therefore seems desirable to keep all musicians together irrespective of whether their primary function is composing, arranging, leading or performing, and irrespective of what instrument they play. It is also difficult to classify precisely every musician by style and this consideration confirms the preference for a single sequence.

Two more important categories are Style and Use. The three major uses have already been discussed in chapter 1 as Functional, Entertainment and Art. For classifying articles, the functional use needs further division so that we can specify dancing and other activities for which jazz has been used as accompaniment. Classification of a given musician or performance by style is often difficult: classification of books or articles rarely so, since they usually come with their own labels. If the list of styles is based on common usage there should be no problem. The obvious order for the arrangement of styles is that of their development.

Apart from a few terms that are peculiar to jazz, the 'technical' categories of Elements, Techniques and Instruments will have a similar content to those used in European music. The main difference will be the order and grouping of instruments. Brass and reeds take precedence in jazz, as compared with strings in European music, and the rhythm section is a grouping peculiar to jazz.

I have distinguished two categories of terms relating to the environment of the music. The first is for the personal, social, economic and legal aspects of the jazz life, the second for activities aimed at the promotion, preservation and dissemination of the music. To these may be added the categories of place and time. Areas and towns of the United States have been arranged in an order that is related to the development of jazz.

For other kinds of Afro-American music I have provided a rather broad classification, since there is no well established detailed one. However, anyone with a particular interest in these forms can expand the section as desired. I am referring, of course, only to the question of which *forms* should be recognized. All other aspects, instruments, environment etc, will be in exactly the same degree of detail as they are for jazz, since any form, Blues, Spirituals etc, may be subdivided by all relevant categories.

A constant source of confusion in classification is the different roles performed by one and the same term. The commonest distinction to be made is between the use of a term to describe the *form* of an item and the use of the same term to describe a *subject*. There are films about jazz and there are writings about films about jazz; there are discographies and writings about discographies; there are opinion polls and writings about opinion polls.

Another important distinction that must be made is that between place and period terms on the one hand and style terms on the other. For example, the modern period in jazz is not synonymous with Modern style, since many earlier styles continue to be played. Jazz in Chicago is not synonymous with Chicago style jazz, since other styles have been played in Chicago: It is possible to have a combination of both elements in one subject, for example one may have an article on the New Orleans style musicians in New Orleans.

All the necessary distinctions have been made in the following scheme, and notes provided to guide the user. Accurate classifying also depends on his ability to analyse the subject of the item in hand.

As a guide to the use of the classification I have given two examples following the schedules and index. The first contains a fair selection of books and demonstrates the order in which they would be arranged on the shelves. The second is an example of an index to periodical articles and essays from collections. It includes many compound subjects and demonstrates the method of combining parts of the notation for this purpose. In particular, the entries under Duke Ellington show just how much detail can be built up from the comparatively short list of elementary terms.

I have provided the fullest detail in classification for those who need it (and this will certainly include some private collectors as well as librarians). For those whose needs are less exacting, appropriate simplifications can obviously be made.

The scheme is based on my own collection and on nearly thirty years of reading in the subject. I am confident that it is sound in essentials, but I know from previous experience that only wide application will reveal minor flaws in a scheme.

Wherever necessary in the following schedules I have put notes of explanation to facilitate their use. The rule for making compound subjects is that the elementary terms are combined in the reverse order of their appearance in the schedules. Thus a study of Duke Ellington as composer would be Sell Nb; the role of the trombone in traditional jazz would be Rg Ph; the neglect of mainstream musicians in the 1960s would be Rn Kk Cl. The only exception to this rule will be found in the treatment of general discographies at class Bg.

The notation has no significance except as a means of preserving the correct order of subjects. It has been allocated in such a way as to keep individual class marks short, and whenever possible to ensure that the most important subjects receive the shortest marks.

A *Physical forms of materials*
To distinguish materials other than books, pamphlets and periodicals. Though the various forms call for separate storage, their index entries may be filed in one sequence. Different coloured cards may be used to indicate the forms.

Do not confuse these form divisions with the same terms used as *subjects* of documents, *eg* Af is for *films* about jazz, Jl is for *writings about* those films.

Ab Scores

Ac Gramophone records (A separate classification for records is given later. This place is provided if required for such things as spoken introductions to jazz, and interviews. For *writings about* records see Jn.)

Ad Tape recordings

Af Films (Writings about films Jl; Jazz as film music Ms.)

Ag Illustrations (May be used for separate illustrations and also to indicate books that consist wholly or mainly of illustrations, *eg* Pictorial history of jazz L Ak.)

Ah Paintings

Aj Drawings

Ak Photographs

Am Programmes
*Imaginative forms*

Ap Collections of more than one form

Ar Humour

As Poetry

At Novels

Av Short stories
It is probably best to group all such works in this section, but they may be classified specifically if desired, *eg* Dorothy Baker's Young man with a horn at Sbei At, or a poem on Billie Holiday at Shol As.

**B** *Reference works, composite works, and introductions*

*Reference works*

General reference works will be classed in this section, while special works will take the notation for the subject, qualified by the appropriate subdivision of B. For example, Rust's *Jazz records A-Z* will be Bg, while his *King Joe Oliver* will be Soli Bg.

If desired, all reference books may be removed from the main sequence and arranged separately.

**Bb** Bibliographies and guides to the literature

**Bbb** Book reviews

**Bc** Dictionaries (Meanings of words used in jazz. For writings on the language of jazz musicians see Kd.)

**Bd** Encyclopedias, Alphabetically arranged reference works including directories of musicians, Handbooks.

**Bf** Pseudonyms of musicians and bands

**Bg** Discographies (For discography as an activity see Jy. This place is for comprehensive discographies. If desired they may be subdivided by period, *eg New hot discography* would be Bg Cc.\*) For discographies of records *issued* in particular countries, divide by D-F. For example, *Jazz catalogue*, Bg Fg.\* For record company catalogues and discographies, further divide alphabetically, *eg* London 'Origins of jazz' catalogue, Bg Fgl. Discographies of records *made* in other countries should be classed with the literature about jazz in particular countries, *eg* Lange, *Die geschichte des jazz in Deutschland*, L Fj Bg. Discographies of individual musicians with writings on the musicians.

**Bh** Selected and annotated record guides

**Bj** Popular, bestselling record lists

**Bk** Record reviews

---

\* Those are the only exceptions to the rule that elementary terms are combined in reverse order of their appearance in the schedule.

**Bm** Surveys, tabulated information (See also **Surveys** as method in research Hh.)

*Composite works*

**Bv** Periodicals

**Bw** Yearbooks

**Bx** Collections of essays by one or more authors (For miscellaneous collections only. Essays on one specific subject do not require this notation, *eg* essays on the history of jazz would be simply **L**.)

*Introductions to jazz*

**By** Primers (Including books for children.)

**Bz** Comprehensive surveys

**C** *Periods*

To be used only as subdivisions of specific subjects. For history use L with the appropriate time division.

If required, years may be specified by adding the following letters to decade notations: b=0, c=1, d=2, f=3, g=4, h=5, j=6, k=7, l=8, m=9.

**Cb** Before the 20th century (Use letters above to specify decade and years if needed.)

**Cc** Early period (*c*1900-*c*1940.)

**Cd** 1900-1920

**Cf** 'Twenties

**Cg** 'Thirties

**Ch** Modern period (For modern style see Rp.)

**Cj** 'Forties

**Ck** 'Fifties

**Cl** 'Sixties

**Cm** 'Seventies

**D-F** *Places*

Use only as subdivisions of specific subjects. History and description of jazz in particular places class at L, with appropriate place divisions.

These schedules are arranged to suit the development of jazz, and prominence is given to the main cities in its history. Other areas of the USA may be specified alphabetically by state and then city, *eg* Boston, Massachusetts would be Dsmb.

D United States of America (Do not use for histories, *eg* Ulanov's *History of jazz in America* will be simply L.)
Dc Southern States, The South
Dd New Orleans (For New Orleans *style* see Rh.)
Df Other states and towns in alphabetical order
Dg South-West
Dh St Louis
Dj Kansas City
Dk Other states and towns in alphabetical order
Dl Middle West
Dm Chicago (For Chicago *style* see Rk.)
Dn Other states and towns in alphabetical order
Dp Eastern States, East-Coast
Dr New York City
Ds Other states and towns in alphabetical order
Dt Western States, West Coast
Dv Los Angeles
Dw San Francisco
Dx Other states and towns in alphabetical order

F The World (exclusive of usa)
Fb America (exclusive of usa)
Fc Latin America
Fcb Mexico
Fcc Central America
Fcj West Indies
Fcr South America
Fd Canada
Ff Europe
Ffb Western Europe
Fg Great Britain
Fh France
Fj Germany
Fk Belgium
Fl Holland
Flc Luxembourg
Fm Switzerland

| | |
|---|---|
| Fn | Austria |
| Fnz | Scandinavia |
| Fp | Norway |
| Fr | Sweden |
| **Fs** | Denmark |
| Fsc | Portugal |
| Fsd | Spain |
| Fsf | Italy |
| Fsg | Greece |
| Fsz | Eastern Europe |
| Ft | Czechoslovakia |
| Ftc | Hungary |
| Ftd | Yugoslavia |
| Ftf | Bulgaria |
| Ftg | Rumania |
| Fth | Poland |
| Ftj | Finland |
| Ftk | Russia |
| Fv | Africa |
| Fvb | West |
| Fvh | North |
| Fvn | East |
| Fvv | South |
| Fw | Asia |
| Fwb | Middle East |
| Fwj | Pakistan |
| Fwk | India |
| Fwm | China |
| Fwp | South-East |
| Fws | Japan |
| Fx | Australia |
| Fy | New Zealand |

**G** *Persons and Institutions*

Use as subdivisions of the appropriate activities, *eg* Collectors Hp Gb, General jazz institutions H Gv, Recording companies Jn Gv.

Gb  Biography and criticism  } Not to be used for jazz
Gc  Autobiography  } musicians—see S
  By age

| Gf | Young |
| Gg | Middle aged |
| Gh | Old |
| | By sex |
| Gj | Man |
| Gk | Woman |
| | By class |
| Gl | Lower |
| Gm | Middle |
| Gn | Upper |
| | By race |
| Gp | Negro |
| Gr | Creole (see also Creole elements Nhd, Creole style Rd.) |
| Gs | White |
| Gv | Institutions, associations, organizations |

| H | *Promotion, Presentation and Dissemination of Jazz* |
| Hc | Research, Musicology (*ie* writings about methods, etc) |
| Hd | Documentary sources |
| Hf | Field Research |
| Hg | Interviews, individual |
| Hh | Questionnaires, polls, surveys (see also Surveys as reference material Bm) |
| Hk | Organization of jazz knowledge |
| Hl | Acquisition of materials, sources, including junk shopping |
| Hm | Classification and indexing |
| Hp | Private collections |
| Hr | Libraries |
| Ht | Museums |
| Hv | Exhibitions |
| Hy | Education (*ie* teaching *about* jazz; training of musicians see Kn) |

| J | Media for performance |
| Jb | Tours |
| Jc | Dancehalls |

| Jd | Nightclubs |
|----|-----------|
| Jf | Brothels |
| Jg | Vaudeville, Minstrel shows, Music-hall |
| Jh | Jazz clubs, Rhythm clubs |
| Jj | Concerts |
| Jk | Festivals |
| Jl | Films (for literature about films with jazz as a subject. For jazz as film music see Ms. For films as physical form see Af.) |
| Jlc | Documentary |
| Jld | Fictional |
| Jm | Radio and Television |
| Jn | Recording |
| Jp | Masters |
| Jr | Takes |
| Js | Records |
| Jt | Issues and reissues |
| Jtd | ' Bootlegging ', ' Pirates ' |
| Jtl | Labels |
| Jtn | Sleeves |
| Jv | 78 rpm |
| Jw | LP, Microgroove |
| Jx | Tape |
| Jy | Discography (as an activity, including writings about discographies. For the discographies themselves see Bg) |

K *Jazz life and environment*
The subdivisions Kc-Kt are for *social* aspects of musicians' lives *in general,* and for any social studies that include both musicians and public. Studies of individual musicians are in class S.

| Kc | Health, dress |
|----|-----------|
| Kd | Language (for dictionaries of jazz terms see Bc) |
| Kf | Psychology—opinions, beliefs, values, attitudes |
| Kg | Attitudes to jazz |
| Kh | Opinions on specific musicians |
| Kj | Recognition, popularity |
| Kk | Neglect |
| Kl | Racial discrimination |

| Km | Addiction |
|---|---|
| Kmb | Alcohol |
| Kmd | Drugs |
| Kn | Training (for jazz as a subject in education see Hy) |
| Kp | Economic factors |
| Kr | Wages and working conditions |
| Ks | Commercialism |
| Kt | Legal factors |
| Kw | Audience, public |

        Divide like Kc-Kt, *eg* Attitudes of public to jazz = Kwg

**Ky** Kinds of audience

        Divide like G, *eg* White audience = Kys

        Divide further as Kw, *eg* Attitudes to jazz of white audience = Kysg

**L** *History*

For periodical articles it is possible to distinguish between the historical and the analytical (which would be classed at M). For books the distinction is not so easy to make and it may be easier to group them all at this point.

    For periods of jazz history divide by C.

    For jazz in particular place divide by D-F.

*Relations with other subjects*

These divisions may also be used to show relations *within* jazz, *eg* the influence of 78 rpm recordings on the form of jazz Nn Lw Jv.

| | | |
|---|---|---|
| Lt | General relationship | *Within* jazz always put earlier notation first in constructing a subject *eg* Comparison of Louis Armstrong and Henry Allen, Sall Lv Sarm |
| Lv | Comparison | |

| | | |
|---|---|---|
| Lw | Jazz influenced by— | *Within* jazz use only Lw See example above, influence of 78 rpm recordings ... |
| Lx | Jazz influencing— | |

Ly  Jazz expounded by—
Lz  Jazz expounding—

M  *The music: description, theory, analysis, criticism*
Mb  Nature of jazz, ' aesthetics '
Mc  Creation, originality
Md  Semantics (implicit or explicit meanings in the music—religious, political, social, sexual, etc). Dictionaries see Bc. Language see Kd
Mf  Emotional qualities
Mg  Modes of expression (romantic, classic, impressionist, expressionist)
Mh  Criticism (*ie* discussion of methods, criteria, viewpoints)
Mj  Uses of jazz
Mk  Functional
Ml  Religious
Mm  Political
Mn  Economics (*eg* advertising)
Mp  Social (*eg* weddings, funerals, house rent parties)
Mr  Dancing
Mrf  Ballet
Ms  Theatre and film accompaniment
Mt  Therapy
Mv  Entertainment
Mw  Art
Mx  ' Jazz and poetry '

N  Techniques of jazz
Nb  Composing
Nba-z  Individual compositions (for subdivision under specific composers only)
Nc  Arranging
Nd  Performing
Ndb  Bandleading
Ndf  Ensemble
Ndj  Solo
Ng  Improvisation
Nh  Elements of jazz

| | |
|---|---|
| Nhb | Historical, origins |
| Nhc | African |
| Nhd | Creole, Latin American (see also Creole persons Gr, Creole style Rd) |
| Nhf | European |
| Nj | Rhythm, Syncopation, Swing |
| Njs | Scales |
| Nk | Melody |
| Nkb | Breaks |
| Nl | Harmony, Polyphony |
| Nm | Timbre |
| Nn | Forms |
| Nnc | Call-and-response |
| Nnd | Riffs |
| Np | Blues (for blues as Afro-American music in their own right see Tg) |
| Nr | Individual blues—arrange in alphabetical order |
| Ns | Rags (for ragtime as Afro-American music in its own right see Tr) |
| Nt | Individual rags—arrange in alphabetical order |
| Nv | Popular songs (for popular music in its own right see V) |
| Nw | Individual songs—arrange in alphabetical order |
| Nx | Classical forms |
| Ny | The ' classics ' (ie specific compositions) |

| | |
|---|---|
| P | *Instruments and bands* |

Instructions for playing a particular instrument will require the addition of Nd, *eg* a jazz piano tutor would be Ps Nd

| | |
|---|---|
| Pb | Bands (Individual bands S) |
| Pc | Big |
| Pd | Small |
| Pdc | Solo instruments (*ie* instruments playing alone —for solos within a group see Ndj) |
| Pdm | Front line, melody instruments |
| Pf | Brass section, brass bands |

| | |
|---|---|
| Pg | Trumpet, cornet |
| Ph | Trombone |
| Phb-z | Others in alphabetical order |
| Pj | Woodwind section |
| Pk | Clarinet |
| Pl | Saxophone |
| Pm | Soprano |
| Pn | Alto |
| Pp | Tenor |
| Ppb | Baritone |
| Ppc | Bass |
| Ppd-z | Others in alphabetical order |
| Pr | String section |
| Prb | Violin |
| Prc-y | Others in alphabetical order |
| Prz | Keyboard instruments |
| Ps | Piano |
| Psb | Organ |
| Psc-z | Others in alphabetical order |
| Pt | Rhythm section |
| Pv | Guitar |
| Pvb | Banjo |
| Pw | Bass, string |
| Pwb | Tuba |
| Px | Percussion, drums |
| Pxa-z | Others in alphabetical order |
| Py | Unorthodox, improvised instruments (*eg* jugs, washboard, kazoos). Arrange in alphabetical order |
| Pz | Voice |

| | |
|---|---|
| R | *Styles of jazz* |
| Rb | Revivals (Use this place for discussions of revivalism in general. For specific revivals use as subdivision of appropriate style *eg* Traditional revival Rg Rb) |
| Rc | Negro |
| Rd | Creole |
| Rf | White |
| Rg | Traditional |

Rc Negro ⎱ (See also Persons, Gp-Gs, Elements Nh)
Rd Creole ⎰

Rh   New Orleans (For jazz *in* New Orleans see Dd)

Rj   Dixieland

Rk   Chicago (For jazz *in* Chicago see Dm)

Rl   South-Western, Kansas City (For jazz *in* the South-West see Dg)

Rm   Harlem (For jazz *in* New York see Dr)

Rn Mainstream (Swing as a style would be Rn Cg, *ie* Mainstream in the 'thirties)

Rp Modern

Rr   Bop, hard bop

Rs   Cool, progressive

Rt Avant Garde

Rw Hybrid styles

Rwb   Afro-Cuban   (For  indigenous  Afro-American music of Cuba see Tt)

Rwc   Third stream

Rwd   Indo-jazz

S *Musicians*

Individual performers, arrangers, composers and bands to be arranged in one alphabetical sequence. Use first three letters of surname, *eg* Louis Armstrong would be Sarm, or more if necessary to distinguish between two similar names.

Books with separate chapters devoted to individual musicians, such as Shapiro and Hentoff's *The jazz makers*, should be classed at S. Books that select musicians according to period, instrument, etc should be classified by the principle of selection, *eg* Williams' *Jazz masters of New Orleans* (*ie* New Orleans style musicians) would be Rh.

For Biography and criticism of individual musicians use S— By.

For Autobiography of individual musicians use S— Bz.

T *Afro-American music*

This section may be subdivided by any appropriate subjects in the preceding jazz schedules, *eg*

Blues discographies Tg Bg, Vocal blues Tg Pz, Piano blues, Boogie-Woogie Tg Ps.

| | |
|---|---|
| Tb | Forms in USA |
| Tc | Religious (Spirituals, gospel songs, etc) |
| Td | Secular (Worksongs, Ringshouts, Hollers, etc) |
| Tf | Folk musicians—arrange in alphabetical order |
| Tg | Blues |
| Th | Country, Southern, Folk |
| Tj | City, Northern |
| Tk | Classic |
| Tl | Rhythm and Blues |
| Tm | Soul |
| Tp | Blues musicians—arrange in alphabetical order |
| Tr | Ragtime |
| Ts | Ragtime musicians—arrange in alphabetical order |
| Tt | Forms in other parts of America |

This section is left for development

V *Popular music*
For twentieth century popular music influenced by Afro-American forms. Specific popularizations and debasements may be indicated by appropriate symbols, *eg* Rock 'n Roll V Tl, Skiffle V Tg Py

Vz Popular musicians in alphabetical order

W *European and other musical traditions*
Use the British Catalogue of Music Classification to provide any detail required in this section.

| | |
|---|---|
| X | *The arts* (excepting music) |
| Xb | Literature |
| Xd | Visual arts |
| Xf | Architecture |
| Xg | Sculpture |
| Xh | Drawing |
| Xj | Painting |
| Xk | Photography |

Xm *The humanities*
Xn   History
Xs   Philosophy
Xw   Religion

Y *Social sciences* (except as provided for in section
*K*) and *Natural sciences*

INDEX TO THE CLASSIFICATION SCHEME

| | |
|---|---|
| Acquisition of materials | Hl |
| Addiction | Km |
| Advertising: Uses of jazz | Mn |
| Africa | Fv |
| African elements | Nhc |
| Afro-American music | T |
| Afro-Cuban jazz | Rwb |
| Alcohol addiction | Kmb |
| Alto saxophone | Pn |
| America | Fb |
| America, Latin | Fc |
| America, United States of | D |
| Architecture | Xf |
| Arranging | Nc |
| Art: Jazz as | Mw |
| Arts | X |
| Asia | Fw |
| Associations | Gv |
| Attitudes | Kf |
| Audience | Kw |
| Australia | Fx |
| Austria | Fn |
| Autobiographies | Gc |
| Avant garde | Rt |
| | |
| Ballet—Jazz for | Mrf |
| Bandleading | Ndb |
| Bands | Pb |
| Banjo | Pvb |
| Baritone saxophone | Ppb |
| Bass (string) | Pw |
| Bass saxophone | Ppc |
| Belgium | Fk |
| Bestselling records | Bj |
| Bibliographies | Bb |
| Big bands | Pc |
| Biographies | Gb |
| Blues: Afro-American music | Tg |
| Blues: Forms in jazz | Np |

| | |
|---|---|
| ' Bootlegging ' records | Jtd |
| Book reviews | Bbb |
| Bop | Rr |
| Brass bands | Pf |
| Brass section | Pf |
| Breaks | Nkb |
| Brothels | Jf |
| Bulgaria | Ftf |
| | |
| Call-and-response | Nnc |
| Canada | Fd |
| Central America | Fcc |
| Chicago (place) | Dm |
| Chicago style | Rk |
| Children: Books for | By |
| China | Fwm |
| City blues | Tj |
| Clarinet | Pk |
| Classes (social) | Gl-Gm |
| Classic blues | Tk |
| Classical forms in jazz | Nx |
| Classical music | W |
| ' Classics ': Jazz use of | Ny |
| Classification | Hm |
| Clubs, Jazz | Jh |
| Clubs, Night | Jd |
| Collecting | Hp |
| Collections: Essays | Bx |
| Collections: Imaginative forms | Ap |
| Commercialism | Ks |
| Communication | Kd |
| Composing | Nb |
| Concerts | Jj |
| Cool jazz | Rs |
| Cornet | Pg |
| Country blues | Th |
| Creation in jazz | Mc |
| Creole elements | Nhd |
| Creole persons | Gr |
| Creole style | Rd |

| | |
|---|---|
| Criticism: Methods etc | Mh |
| Criticism: Of individuals | Gb |
| Czechoslovakia | Ft |
| | |
| Dance halls | Jc |
| Dancing: Jazz for | Mr |
| Denmark | Fs |
| Dictionaries | Bc |
| Directories | Bd |
| Discographies | Bg |
| Discography (activity) | Jy |
| Discrimination, Racial | Kg |
| Dissemination of jazz | H |
| Dixieland | Rj |
| Documentary films | Jlc |
| Documentary sources | Hd |
| Drawing: Art | Xh |
| Drawings: Form of material | Aj |
| Dress | Kc |
| Drug addiction | Kmd |
| Drums | Px |
| | |
| East Africa | Fvn |
| Eastern Europe | Fsz |
| Eastern states: USA | Dp |
| Economic factors | Kp |
| Economics: Uses of jazz | Mn |
| Education in jazz | Hy |
| Elements of jazz | Nh |
| Emotional qualities | Mf |
| Encyclopedias | Bd |
| Ensemble | Ndf |
| Entertainment | Mv |
| Environment | K |
| Essays | Bx |
| Esthetics | Mb |
| Europe | Ff |
| European elements in jazz | Nhf |
| European music | W |
| Exhibitions | Hv |
| Expression, Modes of | Mg |

| | |
|---|---|
| Festivals | Jk |
| Fiction: Films | Jld |
| Fiction: Literature | At |
| Field research | Hf |
| Films about jazz | Jl |
| Films: Form of material | Af |
| Films: Jazz for | Ms |
| Finland | Ftj |
| Folk blues | Th |
| Folk musicians | Tf |
| Forms of jazz | Nn |
| France | Fh |
| Front-line instruments | Pdm |
| Functional jazz | Mk |
| Funerals: Uses of jazz | Mp |
| | |
| Germany | Fj |
| Gospel songs | Tc |
| Gramophone records: Form of material | Ac |
| Gramophone records: Guides | Bh |
| Gramophone records: Media | Js |
| Gramophone records: Reviews | Bk |
| Great Britain | Fg |
| Greece | Fsg |
| Guides to literature | Bb |
| Guides to records | Bh |
| Guitar | Pv |
| | |
| Handbooks | Bd |
| Harlem style | Rm |
| Harmony | Nl |
| Health | Kc |
| Historical elements of jazz | Nhb |
| History (general) | Xn |
| History of jazz | L |
| Holland | Fl |
| Hollers | Td |
| House rent parties | Mp |
| Humanities | Xm |

| | |
|---|---|
| Humour | Ar |
| Hungary | Ftc |
| Hybrid styles | Rw |
| | |
| Illustrations | Ag |
| Imaginative works | Ap-Av |
| Improvisation | Ng |
| Improvised instruments | Py |
| Indexing | Hm |
| India | Fwk |
| Indo-jazz | Rwd |
| Institutions | Gv |
| Instruments | P |
| Interviews | Hg |
| Issues: Records | Jt |
| Italy | Fsf |
| | |
| Japan | Fws |
| ' Jazz and poetry ' | Mx |
| Junkshopping | Hl |
| | |
| Kansas City (place) | Dj |
| Kansas City style | Rl |
| Keyboard instruments | Prz |
| | |
| Labels: Record | Jtl |
| Language | Kd |
| Latin America | Fc |
| Latin American elements in jazz | Nhd |
| Law | Kt |
| Leading (bands) | Ndb |
| Legal factors | Kt |
| Libraries | Hr |
| Literature (general) | Xb |
| Literature of jazz | Bb |
| Longplaying records | Jw |
| Los Angeles | Dv |
| Lower class | Gl |
| Luxembourg | Flc |

| | |
|---|---|
| Mainstream jazz | Rn |
| Masters: Record | Jp |
| Meanings: Music | Md |
| Meanings: Terms | Bc |
| Media for performance | J |
| Melody | Nk |
| Melody instruments | Pdm |
| Men | Gj |
| Mexico | Fcb |
| Microgroove Records | Jw |
| Middle-aged persons | Gg |
| Middle class | Gm |
| Middle East | Fwb |
| Middle West: USA | Dl |
| Minstrel shows | Jg |
| Modern jazz style | Rp |
| Modern period | Ch |
| Museums | Ht |
| Music-hall | Jg |
| Musicians: Afro-American | Tf |
| Musicians: Blues | Tp |
| Musicians: Jazz | S |
| Musicians: Popular | Vz |
| Musicians: Ragtime | Ts |
| Musicians: Social aspects | K |
| Musicology | Hc |
| | |
| Nature of jazz | Mb |
| Neglect of musicians | Kk |
| Negro persons | Gp |
| Negro styles | Rc |
| New Orleans (place) | Dd |
| New Orleans style | Rh |
| New York City | Dr |
| New Zealand | Fy |
| Nightclubs | Jd |
| North Africa | Fvh |
| Northern blues | Tj |
| Norway | Fp |
| Novels | At |

| | |
|---|---|
| Old persons | Gh |
| Opinions | Kf |
| Organ | Psb |
| Organization of jazz knowledge | Hk |
| Organizations | Gv |
| Originality | Mc |
| Origins of jazz | Nhb |
| | |
| Painting: Art | Xj |
| Painting: Form of Material | Ah |
| Pakistan | Fwj |
| Percussion | Px |
| Performing | Nd |
| Periodicals | Bv |
| Periods of jazz | C |
| Persons in jazz | G |
| Philosophy | Xs |
| Photographs: Form of material | Ak |
| Photography: Art | Xk |
| Piano | Ps |
| Pictures: Form of material | Ag |
| ' Pirate ' record companies | Jtd |
| Places of jazz | D-F |
| Poetry: Form of material | As |
| ' Poetry, Jazz and ' | Mx |
| Poland | Fth |
| Political uses of jazz | Mm |
| Polls: Reference material | Bm |
| Polls: Research methods | Hh |
| Polyphony | Nl |
| Popular (bestselling) records | Bj |
| Popular music | V |
| Popular songs: Forms in jazz | Nv |
| Popularity of musicians | Kj |
| Portugal | Fsc |
| Preservation of jazz | H |
| Primers of jazz | By |
| Private collecting | Hp |
| Programmes: Forms of material | Am |

| | |
|---|---|
| Progressive jazz | Rs |
| Promotion of jazz | H |
| Pseudonyms | Bf |
| Psychology | Kf |
| Public | Ky |
| | |
| Questionnaires | Hh |
| | |
| Race of persons | Gp-Gs |
| Racial discrimination | Kl |
| Radio | Jm |
| Rags: Forms in jazz | Ns |
| Ragtime | Tr |
| Recognition of ability | Kj |
| Record guides | Bh |
| Record reviews | Bk |
| Recording | Jn |
| Records: Forms of material | Ac |
| Records: Media | Js |
| Reed instruments | Pj |
| Reference books | B |
| Reissues: Records | Jt |
| Religion | Xw |
| Religious forms: Afro-American music | Tc |
| Religious uses of jazz | Ml |
| Rent parties | Mp |
| Research | Hc |
| Reviews, Book | Bbb |
| Reviews, Record | Bk |
| Revivalism | Rb |
| Rhythm | Nj |
| Rhythm and blues | Tl |
| Rhythm section | Pt |
| Riffs | Nnd |
| Ringshouts | Td |
| Rumania | Ftg |
| Russia | Ftk |
| | |
| St Louis | Dh |
| San Francisco | Dw |

| | |
|---|---|
| Saxophone | Pl |
| Scales | Njs |
| Scandinavia | Fnz |
| Sciences | Y |
| Scores | Ab |
| Sculpture | Xg |
| Secular forms: Afro-American Music | Td |
| Semantics | Md |
| Seventy-eight rpm records | Jv |
| Sleeves: Records | Jtn |
| Small bands | Pd |
| Social aspects of jazz | K |
| Social sciences | Y |
| Social uses of jazz | Mp |
| Solo instruments | Pdc |
| Solo performance | Ndj |
| Songs: Forms in jazz | Nv |
| Soprano saxophone | Pm |
| ' Soul ' Music | Tm |
| South Africa | Fvv |
| South America | Fcr |
| South East Asia | Fwp |
| Southern blues | Th |
| Southern states: USA | Dc |
| South-west states: USA | Dg |
| South-west style | Rl |
| Spain | Fsd |
| Spirituals | Tc |
| Stories, short | Av |
| String bass | Pw |
| String section | Pr |
| Styles of jazz | R |
| Surveys of jazz | Bz |
| Surveys: Reference material | Bm |
| Surveys: Research methods | Hh |
| Sweden | Fr |
| Swing (rhythm) | Nj |
| Swing (style) | Rn Cg |
| Switzerland | Fm |
| Syncopation | Nj |

| | |
|---|---|
| Takes: Recording | Jr |
| Tape recordings: Form of material | Ad |
| Tape recordings: Media | Jx |
| Techniques of jazz | N |
| Television | Jm |
| Tenor saxophone | Pp |
| Theatre: Jazz for | Ms |
| Therapy: Jazz for | Mt |
| Third stream | Rwc |
| Timbre | Nm |
| Tours | Jb |
| Traditional jazz | Rg |
| Training | Kn |
| Trombone | Ph |
| Trumpet | Pg |
| Tuba | Pwb |
| Tune (melody) | Nk |
| Tunes, Blues: in jazz | Np |
| Tunes, Popular: in jazz | Nv |
| Tunes, Ragtime: in jazz | Nr |
| | |
| United States of America | D |
| Unorthodox instruments | Py |
| Upper class | Gn |
| Uses of jazz | Mj |
| | |
| Vaudeville | Jg |
| Violin | Prb |
| Visual arts | Xd |
| Vocal jazz | Pz |
| | |
| Wages | Kr |
| Weddings: Uses of jazz | Mp |
| West Africa | Fvb |
| West Indies | Fcj |
| Western Europe | Ffb |
| Western states: USA | Dt |
| White persons | Gs |
| White styles | Rf |
| Women | Gk |

Woodwind section                               Pj
Working conditions                             Kr
Worksongs                                      Td

Yearbooks                                      Bw
Young persons                                  Gf
Yugoslavia                                     Ftd

*Imaginative works*

| | | |
|---|---|---|
| Poetry | As | Goffin, R *Jazz band* |
| Novels | At | Russell, R *The sound* |
| Stories | Av | Harvey, C *Jazz parody* |

*Reference works*

| | | |
|---|---|---|
| Bibliographies | Bb | Merriam, A *A bibliography of jazz* |
| Dictionaries | Bc | Gold, R S *Jazz lexicon* |
| Encyclopedias and Handbooks | Bd | Panassié, H *Dictionary of jazz* |
| | | Ulanov, B *A handbook of jazz* |
| Pseudonyms | Bf | Rowe, J *Junkshoppers' discography* |
| Discographies | Bg | Rust, B *Jazz records A-Z* |
| | | Jepsen, J G *Jazz records 1942-1967* |
| (by country) | Bg Fg | Cherrington, G *Jazz catalogue* |
| (by firm) | Bg Fgl | Decca Record Company *Complete catalogue of London 'Origins of jazz' records, 1903-1957* |
| Record guides | Bh | McCarthy, A *Jazz on record* |
| (humorous) | Bh Ar | Gammond, P *Fourteen miles on a clear night: an irreverent, sceptical and affectionate book about jazz records* |

*Composite works*

| | | |
|---|---|---|
| Periodicals | Bv | *Jazz monthly* |
| Yearbooks | Bw | Traill, S *(ed) Just jazz* |
| Essays | Bx | Balliett, W *Dinosaurs in the morning* |

*Introductions*

| | | |
|---|---|---|
| Primers | By | Fox, C *Jazz in perspective* |
| Surveys | Bz | Newton, F *The jazz scene* |

*Promotion, etc*

| | | |
|---|---|---|
| Organization of knowledge | Hk | Langridge, D *Your jazz collection* |
| Collectors | Hp Gb Bd | Fry, A *Who's who in jazz collecting* |

| | | |
|---|---|---|
| Films | Jl | Whannel, P *Jazz on film* |
| Record companies | Jn Gv | Wyler, M *A glimpse at the past* |
| *Environment* | K | Hentoff, N *The jazz life* |
| Audience | Kysg D Cc | Leonard, N *Jazz and the white Americans* |
| *History* | L | Stearns, M *The story of jazz* |
| (Illustrated) | L Ak | Keepnews, O *A pictorial history of jazz* |
| Periods | | |
| Early | L Cc | Schuller, G *Early jazz* |
| 'Twenties | L Cf | Hadlock, R *Jazz masters of the 'twenties* |
| 'Thirties | L Cg Ak | Rosencrantz, T *Swing photo album* |
| Modern | L Ch | Wilson, J S *Jazz: the transition years, 1940-1960* |
| 'Forties | L Cj Bd | Dance, S *Jazz era: the forties* |
| Places | | |
| New Orleans | L Dd Bd | Rose, A *New Orleans jazz: a family album* |
| New York | L Dr | Charters, S *Jazz: a history of the New York scene* |
| Great Britain | L Fg | Boulton, D *Jazz in Britain* |
| Germany | L Fj | Lange, H *Jazz in Deutschland* |
| (discography) | L Fj Bg | Lange, H *Die geschichte des jazz in Deutschland* |
| *Techniques* | | |
| Composing | Nb | Russo, W *Jazz composition and orchestration* |
| Performing | Nd | Traill, S *Play that music* |
| Improvising | Ng | Coker, J *Improvising jazz* |
| *Elements* | Nh | Dankworth, A *Jazz: an introduction to its musical basis* |
| *Instruments* | | |
| Big bands | Pc Cg | Simon, G T *The big bands* |
| Piano | Ps | McCarthy, A *(ed) Piano jazz* |
| Piano playing | Ps Nd | Stormen, W *Jazz piano: dixieland to modern jazz* |

| *Styles* | | |
|---|---|---|
| New Orleans | Rh | Williams, M *Jazz masters of New Orleans* |
| Modern | Rp | Horricks, R *These jazzmen of our time* |
| Avant garde | Rt | McRae, B *The jazz cataclysm* |
| *Musicians* | | |
| Collected | S | Shapiro, N *The jazzmakers* |
| (Illustrations) | S Ak | Stock, D *Jazz street* |
| Louis Armstrong | | |
| Discography | Sarm Bg | Jepsen, J G *Discography of Louis Armstrong* |
| Biography and Criticism | Sarm By | McCarthy, A *Louis Armstrong* |
| Autobiography | Sarm Bz | Armstrong, L *Satchmo: my life in New Orleans* |
| *Afro-American music* | T | Courlander, H *Negro folk music, USA* |
| *Blues* | | |
| Discography | Tg Bg | Dixon, R M W *Blues and gospel records 1902-1942* |
| Meanings | Tg Md | Oliver, P *Blues fell this morning* |
| Country | Th | Charters, S *The country blues* |
| Musicians—Broonzy | Tpbro Bz | Broonzy, W *Big Bill blues* |
| *Ragtime* | Tr | Blesh, R *They all played ragtime* |
| *Popular music* | | |
| Encyclopedia | V Bd | Gammond, P *A guide to popular music* |
| Song index | V Bd | Shapiro, N *Popular music: an annotated index of American popular songs* |
| Bestselling records | V Bj | Murrells, J *Daily mail book of golden discs* |
| History | V L | Spaeth, S *A history of popular music in America* |
| Skiffle | V Tg Py | Bird, B *Skiffle, the story of folk song with a jazz beat* |

Musicians
Bing Crosby
    Discography        Vzcro Bg    Mello, E J *Bing Crosby: a discography, 1926-1946*

    Biography         Vzcro By    Ulanov, B *The incredible Crosby*

    Autobiography    Vzcro Bz    Crosby, B *Call me lucky*

*European and other traditions of music*

USA                 W(YT)*    Mellers, W *Music in a new found land*

    New Orleans      W(YTR)*    Kmen, H *Music in New Orleans, the formative years 1791-1841*

    Folk              W/G(YT)*Blesh, R O *Susanna: a sample of the riches of American folk music*

---

\* Notation taken from the British Catalogue of Music Classification.

(Showing the effect of extracting all reference books from the main sequence.)

*General*

| | | |
|---|---|---|
| Bibliographies | Bb | Merriam, A *A bibliography of jazz* |
| Dictionaries | Bc | Gold, R S *Jazz lexicon* |
| Encyclopedias and Handbooks | Bd | Panassié, H *Dictionary of jazz* |
| | | Ulanov, B *A handbook of jazz* |
| Pseudonyms | Bf | Rowe, J *Junkshoppers discography* |
| Discographies | Bg | Rust, B *Jazz records A-Z* |
| | | Jepsen, J G *Jazz records 1942-1965* |
| | Bg Fg | Cherrington, G *Jazz catalogue* |
| | Bg Fgl | Decca Record Company *Complete catalogue of London ' Origin of Jazz' records, 1953-1957* |
| Record guides | Bh | McCarthy, A *Jazz on record* |

*Special*

| | | |
|---|---|---|
| Collectors' directory | Hp Gb Bd | Fry, A *Who's who in jazz collecting* |
| History—illustrations | L Ak | Keepnews, O *A pictorial history of jazz* |
| 'Thirties—illustrations | L Cg Ak | Rosenkrantz, T *Swing photo album* |
| 'Forties—A-Z guide | L Cj Bd | Dance, S *Jazz era: the forties* |
| Germany—discography | L Fj Bg | Lange, H *Die geschichte des jazz in Deutschland* |
| Musicians—illustrations | S Ak | Stock, D *Jazz street* |
| Armstrong—discography | Sarm Bg | Jepsen, J G *Discography of Louis Armstrong* |
| Blues—discography | Tg Bg | Dixon, R M W *Blues and gospel records 1902-1924* |

| Popular—encyclo-<br>pedia | V Bd | Gammond, P *A guide to popular<br>music* |
| Popular—song index | V Bd | Shapiro, N *Popular music: an<br>annotated index of American<br>popular songs* |
| Bestselling records | V Bj | Murrells, J *Daily Mail book of<br>golden discs* |
| Crosby—discography | Vzcro Bg | Mello, E J *Bing Crosby: a disco-<br>graphy, 1926-1946* |

(JJ=*Jazz journal;* JM=*Jazz monthly;* RC=*Record changer.*)

H PROMOTION, PRESERVATION AND DISSEMINATION

H Gb     Promoters

Slatter, M A: 'A portrait of William Russell'. JJ, Sept 1959.

Sullivan, J P: ' John Hammond '. JJ, Sept 1968.

H Gv     Institutions

H Gv D     USA

Harris, S: 'The Institute of Jazz studies'. JJ, Jan 1963.

H Gv Fg     Great Britain

Witherden, B: ' British Institute of Jazz studies '. JM, Feb 1969.

Hk     Organization of knowledge

Hl     Sources of materials

Owen, F: ' The sound of Dobells '. *Storyville* 4.

Hm     Classifying and indexing.

Langridge, D W: ' Classifying the literature of jazz '. *Brio,* Spring 1967.

Hp     Private collections

Grove, T & M: ' Jazz and the collector '. *Jazz review,* 1945.

Hp Gb     Collectors

Carey, D: ' Young collector's guide to other collectors '. JJ, June 1949.

James, M: ' Profile of a collector '. JM, Sept 1960.

Hp Gv     Institutions

'International Association of Jazz Record Collectors '. *Storyville* 21.

Hr     Libraries

Langridge, D W: ' Jazz and libraries'. *The library world,* March 1966.

Ht     Museums

Ht Dd     New Orleans

New Orleans Jazz Club: *New Orleans Jazz Museum: 5th anniversary celebration.* 1966.

Hy     Education

Stearns, M: ' Jazz: an elective course '. RC, June 1952.

J MEDIA FOR PERFORMANCE

Jb Gv    Touring organizations
Granz, N: ' Jazz at the Philharmonic '. In Traill,
S *(ed)*: *Just jazz 2*, 1958.

Jd    Nightclubs
Jd Dr    New York
Hoefer, G: ' Cafe society downtown and up-
town '. In *Downbeat music '67*.

Jj    Concerts
Newton, F: ' Jazz concerts '. In Williamson, K
*(ed)*: *This is jazz*, 1960.

Jj D    USA
Morgan, A: ' The second and third *Esquire* jazz
concerts '. JM, Jan 1967.

Jl    Films
Morgenstern, D: ' Jazz on film '. In *Downbeat
music '67*

Jn    Recording
Jn Gv    Companies
Record labels in jazz history '. In *The jazzfinder
'49*.

Jr    Takes
Peterson, O: ' Masters and masterpieces '. JJ, Aug
1967.

Js    Records
Jt    Issues
Jt Fg    Great Britain
McCarthy, A: ' The future of jazz releases in this
country '. JM, Sept 1966.

Jtd    ' Pirates '
Smith, C E: ' Background to bootlegging '. RC,
Jan 1952.

Jw    LPS
Turley, P: ' Jazz and the long-playing record '.
JM, Aug 1958.

Jy    Discography
Gronow, P: ' Discography as a science '.JM, Aug
1968.

**K JAZZ, LIFE AND ENVIRONMENT**
**Kd**     Language
Ulanov, B: 'The language of jazz'. In *A handbook of jazz*, 1958.

**Kj**     Recognition, popularity
Hodeir, A: 'Popularity or recognition?' In *Toward jazz*, 1962.

**Kk**     Neglect
Standish, T: 'Gold in the junkyards'. In Traill, S (*ed*): *Just jazz 3*, 1959.

**Kl**     Racial discrimination
Griffiths, D: 'Jazz and racial discrimination'. JM, May 1956.

**Km**    Addiction
Winick, C: 'The taste of music: alcohol, drugs and jazz'. JM, Oct/Nov 1962.

**Kp**     Economic factors
Feather, L: 'The money of making art'. JM, Sept 1958.

**Kw**    The audience
Newton, F: 'The public'. In *The jazz scene*, 1959.

**Kwg**       Attitudes
**Kwg D Cf**       USA 1920's
Leonard, N: 'The opposition to jazz in the US 1918-1929'. JM, June/July 1958.

**Kwh**       Opinions on musicians
**Kwh Fg**       England
**Kwh Fg Ckl Bm**       1958
'Poll results 1958'. In Traill, S (*ed*): *Just jazz 3*, 1959.

**Kwh Hj**    Opinion polls
Lascelles, G: 'Popularity polls'. In Traill, S (*ed*): *Just jazz 2*, 1958.

**L** HISTORY
Williams, M: 'Last trip up the river'. JJ, Oct 1965.

**L Cg**    'Thirties
Fox, C: 'The end of an era'. In McCarthy, A (*ed*): *Jazzbook 1955*.

L Dd    New Orleans
Miller, P E: ' Fifty years of New Orleans jazz '. In *Esquire's 1945 jazz book.*

LDd Cld    1962
Lucas, J: ' New Orleans 1962 '. JJ, Sept 1962.

L Dh    St Louis
L Dh Ckl    1958
Koester, B: ' Jazz in St Louis—1958 '. In Traill S *(ed)*: *Just jazz 2,* 1958.

L Dm    Chicago
Miller, P E: ' Thirty years of Chicago jazz '. In *Esquire's 1946 jazz book.*

L Dm Cf    'Twenties
Reeves, E M: ' Chicago in the 'twenties '. JJ, Apr/May 1961.

L Dsmb    Boston
Napoleon, A: ' Bunker Hill, baked beans and Braff '. JJ, Feb 1968.

L Dt    West Coast
L Dt Cf    'Twenties
Bentley, J: ' West coast jazz in the 'twenties '. JM, May 1961.

L Fg    Great Britain
Wilford, C: ' Jazz over England '. In McCarthy, A *(ed)*: *PL yearbook of jazz 1946.*

L Fwk    India
Brown, K: ' Jazz in India '. *Jazz forum* no 2.

L Fx    Australia
Miller, W H: ' The position of jazz in Australia '. *Jazz forum no 2.*

Lt-Lx    JAZZ IN RELATION TO OTHER SUBJECTS
Lt V Tl    Jazz and rock n' roll
Delehart, J: ' Is jazz going longhair?' In *Downbeat music '67.*

Lt W    Jazz and European music
James, B: ' On swinging Bach '. In *Essays on jazz,* 1961.

Lv Xb    Jazz compared to poetry
Moore, N: ' Notes on jazz and poetry'. *Jazz forum no 2.*

Ly Xd    Jazz in the visual arts
Leonard, A: ' Jazz philately '. JJ, May 1969.
Oliver, P: 'Art aspiring '. JM, Feb 1957.


M THE MUSIC
Mb    Nature of jazz
Feather, L: ' Whatever happened to beauty—or,
Who wants pleasant music?' In *Downbeat music
'67.*
Mc    Originality and creation
Hodeir, A: 'Why do they age so badly?' In
*Toward jazz*, 1962.
Moore, N: ' In defence of originality '. In *PL
yearbook of jazz 1946.*
Mf    Emotional qualities
Dare, A: ' Sentimentality and jazz '. RC, Dec 1952.
Mh    Criticism
Hodeir, A: ' On criticism '. Part 2 of *Toward
jazz*, 1962.
Mh Gb    Critics
Lyttleton, H: ' Critic v musician '. In Traill, S
(*ed*): *Just jazz 3*, 1959.
Mj    USES OF JAZZ
Mr    Dancing
Dodge, R P: ' The dance basis of jazz '. In
McCarthy, A (*ed*): *PL jazzbook 1947.*
Ms    Film music
Shaw, R B: 'Anatomy of film jazz '. In Traill, S
(*ed*): *Just jazz 4*, 1960.
Mw    Art
McCarthy, A: ' Jazz as art?' In Traill, S (*ed*):
*Just jazz, 4*, 1960.
Mx    ' Jazz and poetry '
Fox, C: ' Red bird dancing on ivory: some
aspects of jazz and poetry '. JM, June 1960.


N TECHNIQUES OF JAZZ
Hodeir, A: ' Freedom and its limitations in
improvisation and composition '. In *Toward jazz*,
1962.

Nb    Composing
Harrison, M: 'Notes on jazz composition'. JM, Apr 1963.

Ndf    Ensemble playing
Dodge, R P: 'The deceptive nature of sensuousness in ensemble playing'. In McCarthy, A (*ed*): *PL yearbook of jazz 1946*.

Ndj    Solo playing
Fox, C: 'Concerning the hot solo'. *Jazz forum no 2*.

Ng    Improvisation
James, B: 'The art of improvisation'. In *Essays on jazz*, 1961.

Nh  ELEMENTS OF JAZZ

Nhc    African
Blesh, R: 'Chart showing African survivals in Negro jazz'. In *Shining trumpets*, 1949.

Nhd    Creole
Borneman, E: 'Creole echoes'. In Traill, S (*ed*): *Just jazz 2*, 1958.

Nhf    European
Thompson, K: 'The Western heritage of jazz'. RC, Apr 1950.

Nj    Rhythm, Swing
Locke, D: 'Swinging: an analysis of the jazz rhythm'. JM, Apr/May 1963.

Nn    Forms
Kington, M: 'Form in jazz if any'. JJ, Mar/Apr 1967.

Nn Lw Jv    Influenced by 78rpm recordings
Cooke, J: 'Forty years in a straightjacket: a dissenting opinion on the three minute form'. JM, Dec 1960.

Np Cc    Blues form in early jazz
Munnery, P: 'The blues form and its influence on early jazz'. JJ, Sept 1967.

Np Lw Jv    Influenced by 78rpm recordings
Williams, M: 'Recording limits and blues form'. In *The art of jazz*, 1960.

Nrt Bg      Tin Roof Blues—Discography
McGeagh, M: ' Discography of Tin Roof Blues '.
JJ, Feb 1950.

Ns      Rags

Ntt Bg      Tiger Rag—Discography
Madison, J: ' Discography of Tiger Rag '. RC,
Apr 1949.

Nv      Popular song
Littler, F: ' King Porter and Miss Annabelle
Lee '. JM, July 1958.

Ny      The ' classics '
Harrison, M: ' Jazzing the classics '. JM, Aug 1965.

P INSTRUMENTS
Harrison, M: ' New instruments on new paths '.
JM, Jan 1958.

Pc    Big bands
Fox, C: ' The development of orchestral jazz '.
In *PL yearbook of jazz 1946*.

Pd    Small bands
Houlden. D: ' The development of small-band
jazz styles '. JJ, Feb/Mar 1949.

Pg    Trumpet
Dare, A: ' Cornet and trumpet: some notes on
use and history '. RC, Oct 1950.

Pl    Saxophone
Roth, R: ' The saxophone: an analysis '. RC,
Feb/Apr 1951.

Ps    Piano
Ellington, D: ' The most essential instrument '.
JJ, Dec 1965.

Px    Drums
Roth, R: ' Drums: an analysis '. RC, Sept 1951.
Voice

Pz Locke, D: ' The jazz vocal '. JM, Sept 1967.

R STYLES
Lyttelton, H: ' The common denominator '. In
Traill, S (*ed*): *Just jazz 2*, 1958.

Rf   White

Lucas, J: 'The great white way'. In Traill, S (ed): *Just jazz 4*, 1960.

Rf Np   Blues

Fox, C: 'Blues and the white musicians'. JM, Sept 1960.

Rg Rb   Traditional revival

Allen, W C: 'The revival appraised'. JJ, Sept 1962.

Rg Rb Lt Rk   In relation to Chicago style

Standish, T: 'Reflections in a dusty mirror'. JM, Dec 1958.

Rh   New Orleans

King, B: 'A reassessment of New Orleans jazz on American Music records'. JM, Mar/Apr 1959.

Rh Pg   Trumpeters

Carey, M: 'New Orleans trumpet players'. *Jazz music* Vol 3, no 4.

Rj   Dixieland

Keepnews, O: 'Dixieland'. In Williams, M (*ed*): *The art of jazz*, 1960.

Rk   Chicago

Lambert, G: 'Reflections on jazz history and the Chicagoans'. JM, Aug/Sept 1958.

Rk Pk   Clarinettists

Patterson, J: 'Chicago style clarinet'. RC, July 1952.

Rm Ps Mp   Harlem—Pianists—House rent parties

Bright, K: 'Parlour social'. In McCarthy, A (*ed*): *PL jazzbook 1947*.

Rn   Mainstream

Fenby, J: 'The new revivalists'. JJ, Aug 1960.

Rn Jt   Record issues

Postgate, J: 'Mainstream jazz: issues and re-issues'. JM, Oct 1966.

Rp   Modern

Harrison, M: 'Never mind the music'. JM, Nov 1959.

Rr    Bop

Russell, R: ' Bebop '. In Williams, M: *The art of jazz*, 1960.

Rt    Avant garde

Williams, M: ' The new thing '. In *Where's the melody?* 1966.

Rwc    Third stream

Pekar, H: ' Third stream jazz '. JJ, Dec 1962.

Rwd    Indo-jazz

Graham, V: ' Indo-jazz '. *Audio record review*, Apr 1969.

S MUSICIANS

Sell Duke Ellington

Sell Bh    Record guides

Lambert, G E: ' The essential Ellington on French RCA'. JM, Oct 1964

Sell By    Biography and criticism

Bellerby, V: ' Duke Ellington '. In Williams, M (*ed*): *The art of jazz*, 1960.

Heughan, G: 'An historical calendar of Duke Ellington's career '. JJ Jan 1963.

Sharpe, D: 'An appreciation of Duke Ellington '. JJ, Oct 1956.

Williams, M: ' The genesis of Duke '. JJ, Feb 1965.

Sell Bz    Autobiography

Ellington, Duke: ' Reminiscing in tempo '. JJ, Feb 1967.

Sell C    Periods

Sell Cg    'Thirties

Fox, C: ' Duke Ellington in the 'thirties '. In Williams, M (*ed*): *The art of jazz*, 1960.

Sell Cjg    1944

Feather, L: ' Duke Ellington—1944 '. *Discography no 4*, 1944.

Sell Cjm    1949

Otto, A: ' The Duke at the half-century mark '. JJ, Feb 1950.

Sell Jb    Tours

Sell Jb Fg    Great Britain

Sell Jb Fg Clf Lambert, E: 'Duke Ellington—1963'. JJ, Mar 1963.

Sell Jb Fg ClfAm Davison, H and Granz, N: 'Present Duke Ellington and his famous orchestra in concert' (1963 tour programme).

Sell Jb Fg Clg Lambert, G: 'Ellingtonia '64'. JJ, Apr 1964.

Sell JbFgClgAm Davison, H and Granz, N: 'Present Duke Ellington and his famous orchestra in concert'. (1964 tour programme).

Sell Jb Fwj     Pakistan

Sell Jb Fwj Clf Craik, R: 'Duke in Dacca'. JJ, Jan 1964.

Sell Jn     Recording
Townsend, I: 'When Duke Records'. In Traill, S (ed): *Just jazz 4*, 1960.

Sell Mg     Mode of expression
Bellerby, V: 'Reflections on Duke Ellington—4 The delicate impressionist'. JM, Apr 1956.
James, B: 'The impressionism of Duke Ellington'. In *Essays on jazz*, 1961.

Sell Nb     Composing
Harrison, M: 'Duke Ellington: reflections on some of the larger works'. JM, Jan 1964.
Compositions

Sell Nbc Bishop, A: 'Duke's Creole rhapsody'. JM, Nov 1963.

Sell Nbh Horricks, R: 'Duke Ellington and the Harlem suite'. JM, July 1956.

Sell Nbk Js Hodeir, A: 'Why did Duke Ellington remake his masterpiece?' (Ko-Ko). In *Toward jazz*, 1962.

Sell Nbr Bishop, A: 'Reminiscing in tempo'. JJ, Feb 1964.

Sell Nbs James, B: 'Such sweet thunder'. In *Essays on jazz*, 1961.

Sell P     Instruments

Sell Pd     Small bands
Pekar, H: 'The Duke Ellington small bands'. JJ, Jan 1963.

Sell Pg     Trumpet section

Sell Pg Ckl Lambert, G: 'Trumpets no end'. JJ, Jan 1961.

Sell Px     Drummers

Ioakimidis, D: 'Ellington's drummers'. JJ, Jan 1963.

T   AFRO-AMERICAN MUSIC

Tb    USA

Korner, A: 'Ragtime, ringshouts, and hollers'. In McCarthy, A (ed): *Jazzbook 1955*.

Tb Bb      Bibliography

Oliver, P: 'Literature on Negro folk song'. JM, Feb 1966.

Tc    Religious

Hurston, Z: 'Spirituals and neo-spirituals'. In McCarthy, A (ed): *PL jazzbook 1947*.

Td    Secular

Preston, D: 'The poetry of American negro folksong: worksongs'. In McCarthy, A (ed) *PL jazzbook 1947*.

Tg    Blues

Borneman, E: 'The blues: a study in ambiguity'. In Traill, S (ed): *Just jazz 3* 1959.

Tg Mh      Criticism

Gruver, R: 'Towards a criticism of the blues'. JM, Jan 1968.

Tg Ps    Boogie woogie

Borneman, E: 'Boogie-woogie', In Traill, S (ed): *Just jazz*, 1957.

Tg Pz    Singers

Tg Pz Bf      Pseudonyms

Owen, F: 'The name's not the same'. *Storyville* 1 and 2.

Tg Pz Dm      Chicago

Bruynoghe, Y: 'Chicago, home of the blues'. In Traill, S (ed): *Just jazz 2*, 1958.

Th Pz    Country blues

Stewart-Baxter, D: 'Blues in the country'. JJ, Apr 1959.

Tl    Rhythm and blues

McCarthy, A: 'Rhythm and blues'. In *Jazzbook 1955*.

<dl>
<dt>Tp</dt><dd>Musicians</dd>
<dt>Tpbro</dt><dd>Big Bill Broonzy</dd>
<dt>Tpbro Bg</dt><dd>Discography</dd>
</dl>

McCarthy, A: 'Discography of Big Bill Broonzy'. *Jazz forum no 4.*

<dl>
<dt>Tpbro Bz</dt><dd>Autobiography</dd>
</dl>

Broonzy, W: 'Blues in 1890'. In McCarthy, A (*ed*): *Jazzbook 1955.*

<dl>
<dt>Tr</dt><dd>Ragtime</dd>
<dt>Tr Bg</dt><dd>Discography</dd>
</dl>

Carey, D: 'Listing of ragtime recordings'. JJ, Feb 1950.

<dl>
<dt>Tr Dfms</dt><dd>Sedalia</dd>
</dl>

Campbell, S: 'Sedalia, Missouri, cradle of ragtime'. In McCarthy, A (*ed*): *PL jazzbook 1947.*

<dl>
<dt>Tr Js</dt><dd>Records</dd>
</dl>

Spottswood, R: 'Discoveries concerning recorded ragtime'. JJ, Feb 1968.

<dl>
<dt>Tr M</dt><dd>Musical analysis</dd>
</dl>

Waterman, G: 'Ragtime'. In Williams, M (*ed*): *The art of jazz*, 1960.

<dl>
<dt>Ts</dt><dd>Musicians</dd>
<dt>Ts Gs</dt><dd>White</dd>
</dl>

Campbell, S: 'Early great white ragtime composers and pianists'. JJ, May 1949.

<dl>
<dt>Tslam</dt><dd>Joseph Lamb</dd>
</dl>

Cassidy, R: 'Joseph Lamb—last of the ragtime composers'. JM, Aug, Oct, Nov, Dec, 1961.

## V POPULAR MUSIC

<dl>
<dt>V Pz</dt><dd>Singers</dd>
</dl>

Dodge, R: 'Popular singers'. JM, July 1959.

<dl>
<dt>V Pz Md</dt><dd>Meanings</dd>
</dl>

Ward, C: 'Sing me a song of social significance'. JM, May 1958.

<dl>
<dt>V T Py</dt><dd>Skiffle</dd>
</dl>

Green, B: 'The usurpers'. In Traill, S (*ed*): *Just jazz 2*, 1958.

Acquisition of materials — Hl
Addiction — Kh
African elements — Nhc
Afro-American music — T
Art: Jazz as — Mw
Arts: Expounding jazz — Ly X
Attitudes: Audience — Kwg
Audience — Kw
Australia: History: Jazz — L Fx
Autobiography: Broonzy — Tpbro Bz
Autobiography: Ellington — Sell Bz
Avant garde — Rt

Big bands — Pc
Biography: Ellington — Sell By
Blues: Afro-American music — Tg
Blues: Form in jazz — Np
Blues: White musicians — Rf Np
Boogie-woogie — Tg Ps
Bop — Rr
Boston: History: Jazz — L Dsmb
British Institute of Jazz Studies — H Gv Fg
Broonzy, Big Bill — Tpbro

Café Society — Jd Dr
Chicago: Blues singers — Tg Pz Dm
Chicago: History: Jazz — L Dm
Chicago style — Rk
Chicago style: In relation to traditional revival — Rg Rb Lt Rk
Clarinet: Chicago style — Rk Pk
' Classics ': Jazz treatment — Ny
Classification: Jazz literature — Hm
Collecting — Hp
Collectors — Hp Gb
Companies: Recording — Jn Gv
Composing — Nb
Composing: Ellington — Sell Nb
Concerts — Jj
Cornet — Pg

| | |
|---|---|
| Country blues | Th |
| Creation in jazz | Mb |
| Creole elements in jazz | Nhd |
| *Creole rhapsody* | Sell Nbc |
| Criticism: Blues | Tg Mh |
| Criticism: Jazz | Mh |
| Critics | Mh Gb |
| | |
| Dancing: Jazz for | Mr |
| Discography | Jy |
| Discography: Broonzy | Tpbro Bg |
| Discography: Ragtime | Tr Bg |
| Discography: *Tiger Rag* | Ntt Bg |
| Discography: *Tin Roof Blues* | Nrt Bg |
| Discrimination, Racial | Kl |
| Dixieland style | Rj |
| Dobell's Jazz Record Shop | Hl |
| Drums | Px |
| Drums: Ellington | Sell Px |
| | |
| Economics: Jazz life | Kp |
| Education: Jazz | Hy |
| Elements of jazz | Nh |
| Ellington, Duke | Sell |
| Emotional qualities: Jazz | Mf |
| Ensemble playing | Ndf |
| Esquire Jazz Concerts | Jj D |
| Esthetics | Mb |
| European elements of jazz | Nhf |
| European music—in relation to jazz | Lt W |
| | |
| Films on jazz | Jl |
| Films: Jazz for | Ms |
| Forms of jazz | Nn |
| | |
| Great Britain: History: Jazz | L Fg |
| Great Britain: Institutions | H Gv Fg |
| Great Britain: Record issues | Jt Fg |
| Great Britain: Tours: Ellington | Sell Jb Fg |

| | |
|---|---|
| Hammond, John | H Gb |
| Harlem style | Rm |
| *Harlem suite* | Sell Nbh |
| History: Jazz | L |
| House rent parties: Piano: Harlem style | Rm Ps Mp |
| | |
| Impressionism: Ellington | Sell Mg |
| Improvisation | Ng |
| India: History: Jazz | L Fwk |
| Indo-jazz | Rwd |
| Institute of Jazz Studies | H Gv D |
| Institutions: Collectors | Hp Gv |
| Institutions: Jazz | H Gv |
| Instruments | P |
| Instruments: Ellington | Sell P |
| International Association of Jazz Record Collectors | Hp Gv |
| Issues: Records | Jt |
| Issues: Records: Mainstream | Rn Jt |
| | |
| ' Jazz and poetry ' | Mx |
| Jazz at the Philharmonic | Jb Gv |
| | |
| *Ko-Ko* | Sell Nbk |
| | |
| Lamb, Joseph | Tslam |
| Language | Kd |
| Libraries | Hr |
| Longplaying records | Jw |
| | |
| Mainstream style | Rn |
| Meanings: Popular songs | V Pz Md |
| Media for jazz | J |
| Modern style | Rp |
| Museums | Ht |
| Musicians: Blues | Tp |
| Musicians: Jazz | S |
| Musicians: Ragtime | Ts |

| | |
|---|---|
| Neglected musicians | Kk |
| New Orleans: History: Jazz | L Dd |
| New Orleans Jazz Museum | Ht Dd |
| New Orleans style | Rh |
| New York: Nightclubs | Jd Dr |
| Nightclubs | Jd |
| | |
| Opinions on musicians: Audience | Kwh |
| Organization of jazz knowledge | Hk |
| Originality in jazz | Mb |
| | |
| Pakistan: Tours: Ellington | Sell Jb Fwj |
| Philately: Jazz subjects | Ly Xd |
| Piano | Ps |
| Piano: Harlem style | Rm Ps |
| ' Pirate ' record issues | Jtd |
| ' Poetry, Jazz and ' | Mx |
| Poetry: Compared to jazz | Lv Xb |
| Poll results: 1958: Great Britain | Kwh Fg Ckl Bm |
| Polls: Opinions: Audience | Kwh Hh |
| Popular music | V |
| Popular songs: Form in jazz | Nv |
| Popularity: Musicians | Kj |
| Private collections | Hp |
| Promoters | H Gb |
| Pseudonyms: Blues singers | Tg Pz Bf |
| Public | Kw |
| | |
| Racial discrimination | Kl |
| Rags: Form in jazz | Ns |
| Ragtime | Tr |
| Recognition of ability | Kj |
| Record guides: Ellington | Sell Bh |
| Recording | Jn |
| Recording: Ellington | Sell Jn |
| Records | Js |
| Records: *Ko-Ko* | Sell Nbk Js |
| Records: Mainstream | Rn Js |
| Records: Ragtime | Tr Js |
| Religious forms: USA: Afro-American music | Tc |

| | |
|---|---|
| *Reminiscing in tempo* | Sell Nbr |
| Rent parties: Piano: Harlem style | Rm Ps Mp |
| Revival: Traditional jazz | Rg Rb |
| Rhythm | Nj |
| Rhythm and blues | Tl |
| Rock n' roll: In relation to jazz | Lt V Tl |
| Russell, William | H Gb |
| | |
| St Louis: History: Jazz | L Dh |
| Saxophone | Pl |
| Secular forms: USA: Afro-American music | Td |
| Sedatia: Ragtime | Tr Dfms |
| Seventy eight rpm recordings: Influencing blues form | Np Lw Jv |
| Seventy eight rpm recordings: Influencing form in jazz | Nn Lw Jv |
| Singers: Blues | Tg Pz |
| Singers: Country blues | Th Pz |
| Singers: Jazz | Pz |
| Singers: Popular music | V Pz |
| Skiffle: Popular music | V T Py |
| Small bands | Pd |
| Small bands: Ellington | Sell Pd |
| Solo playing | Ndj |
| Sources for jazz materials | Hl |
| Spirituals | Tc |
| Styles: Jazz | R |
| *Such sweet thunder* | Sell Nbs |
| Swing (rhythm) | Nj |
| | |
| Takes: Recording | Jr |
| Techniques of jazz | N |
| Third stream | Rwc |
| 'Thirties: History: Jazz | L Cg |
| *Tiger rag* | Ntt |
| *Tin roof blues* | Nrt |
| Touring organizations | Jb Gv |
| Tours: Ellington | Sell Jb |
| Traditional jazz | Rg |
| Trumpet | Pg |

Trumpet: New Orleans style                    Rh Pg
Trumpet section: Ellington                    Sell Pg
'Twenties: Chicago                            L Dm Cf
'Twenties: West Coast                         L Dt Cf

USA: Afro-American music                       Tb
USA: Attitudes to jazz: Audience               Kwg D
USA: Concerts                                  Jj D
USA: Institutions                             H Gv D
Uses of jazz                                   Mj

Visual arts: Expounding jazz                   Ly Xd
Vocal jazz                                     Pz

West Coast: History: Jazz                      L Dt
White musicians: Ragtime                       Ts Gs
White styles: Jazz                             Rf
Worksongs                                      Td

READINGS FOR CHAPTER THREE

1 *Indexing—general and music literature*

Coates, E J: *Subject catalogues.* Library Association, 1960 (esp chapter IX).

Foskett, A C: *The subject approach to information.* Bingley, 1969.

Knight, G N (*ed*): *Training in indexing.* MIT Press, 1969.

Needham, C D: *Organizing knowledge in libraries.* Deutsch, 1964.

Redfern, B: *Organizing music in libraries.* Bingley, 1966.

2 *Classification of jazz literature*

Coates, E J: *The British Catalogue of Music Classification.* British National Bibliography, 1960.

Langridge, D W: 'Classifying the literature of jazz'. *Brio*, Spring 1967.

# *The collection—2 arrangement and indexing of records*

ARRANGEMENT OF THE RECORDS: I shall not refer to storage equipment, for this has been dealt with adequately in other publications. The only physical factor affecting arrangement is the need to keep different sizes of records in separate sequences. The ideal would obviously be one sequence, but the jazz collector is likely to be further from this objective than most: a collection of any size will almost certainly include 78s and three sizes of microgroove. The records themselves need not be marked, as it is self-evident where they belong, but any index to the collection would have to indicate the appropriate sequence for each record. Apart from this, the problem need not concern us; all sizes of records can be arranged in a similar way.

The purpose of systematic arrangement is the quick and certain finding of any item or items. When the collection is very small this may be no problem, but the most important piece of advice that can be given to beginners is to plan for growth. It is reasonably easy to organize a collection from the beginning. To do the same for a well-established collection calls for an amount of time and patience that few are able to give. I shall therefore assume that we are concerned with collections that either are, or will be, beyond the size where it is practicable to examine every record to find what we want.

Records are like books in that they may be approached in a variety of ways. For example, we may want one or all of the recordings of a particular band or soloist; we may want all the records in which a particular musician takes part; we may want all the recordings of a particular theme or all the recordings of themes written by a particular composer, and so on. The arrangement of the records themselves cannot deal with all these approaches, so that an index is essential to reveal the scope of a collection. Indexing is dealt with later in this chapter. For the moment the question is whether the record arrangement should attempt to group the records in such a way that at least one kind of approach may be made without recourse to the index. The alternative is to arrange by a method which is purely a finding convenience but has no significance in relation to the contents of the record.

## RECORD NUMBERS AND ACCESSION NUMBERS

There are two such methods. One can either make use of the manufacturers' own identification numbers, or one can assign a running number to each record as it is added to the collection. The first is supposedly the simpler as the record already has its number when purchased, and no further marking of the cover is necessary. In practice this advantage is likely to disappear since there is no standard position for printing the number on record covers. Many do not have the number on the spine, and even when they do the numbers appear in a variety of positions and may run upwards or downwards. For convenience of finding, the collector would have to mark each cover in a standard position. The best method of doing this is to affix a small self-adhesive label either to the top right-hand corner of the back of the cover or the top left-hand corner of the front. The chief disadvantage of the method for the private collector is that the record's number is the characteristic he is least likely to remember, and he will therefore have to use the index more frequently than with other methods. For libraries that do not allow their users direct access to the records the position is different. The index would have to be used here in any case, so for them it may well be the most suitable method. I can see nothing to recommend it to the private collector or to the library that does allow direct access to records.

The advantages claimed for the running (or accession) number method are that it requires no disturbance of the records as new ones are added, and that it shows the development of the collector's taste and interest. The former strikes me as a comparatively unimportant matter, while the latter advantage can be obtained without arranging the records in this way. If the collector is interested in the growth aspect he can cater for it better by recording his purchases in a notebook where it is possible to add as much information as he likes—place of purchase, price, date and reason for selling, etc. In comparison with the previous method, one is certainly likely to remember more easily where a record is in such a sequence, and it does ensure that the latest purchase (and therefore probably for the moment the most frequently played) is the most easily accessible. These advantages and the simplicity of the method may well recommend it to some collectors, but there will be many who prefer to arrange their records by some characteristic of the music itself. To these methods I now turn.

ARRANGEMENT BY PERFORMER

The objective now is to arrange the records so that one kind of approach is possible without using the index—the commonest approach being the obvious choice. In classical music this would be the name of the composer; in jazz it would be the composer's equivalent, the performing group or soloist. In theory this method is simple enough; in practice it presents two kinds of difficulty. The first concerns the name of the group. Records are not always reissued under the same name as the original, for example the Kansas City Five recordings of 1938 and 1944 were reissued on Stateside as Lester Young and the Kansas City Five. The discographies discussed in chapter 2 may be used to establish the correct name, but this does not solve all problems. Many bands recorded under a variety of names. Fletcher Henderson groups, for example, not only appeared under Henderson's name, but also as the Dixie Stompers, the Louisiana Stompers, Baltimore Bell Hops, Connie's Inn Orchestra, the Stokers of Hades, and Horace Henderson and his Orchestra. In a collection of 78s it would be possible to arrange by original recording names, but it doesn't seem very helpful to split up the records of what is essentially one group. With LPs the method is not even feasible. The CBS four volume ' Study of frustration ', for example, contains recordings made under more than one of the names used by Henderson groups. The only solution is to use a standard name, in this case ' Fletcher Henderson '. This is the method adopted by the Carey-McCarthy discography, *Jazz directory*. Unfortunately it is incomplete, but will serve as a guide as far as it goes.

The second kind of difficulty arises from the heterogeneous nature of the contents of many jazz records. The only collection avoiding this problem would be one consisting solely of first edition 78s. Reissue 78s were notorious for their mixed couplings —Louis Armstrong with Joe Venuti, Earl Hines with Eddie Lang, Luis Russell with Jack Purvis and so on. Short of buying duplicate copies, one can only put one side in its proper place and leave the index to find the other. With LPs the scope for variety of contents is greater. If only two groups are included, as on the Italian RCA ' Mezzin' around ' (Mezzrow's Swing Band and Frankie Newton's Orchestra), the treatment can be similar to that for 78s. Collections of more than two groups may be based on several different characteristics: the work of a particular musician, eg Riverside's ' Tommy Ladnier blues and stomps ', Storyville's ' George Lewis with Kid Shots' New Orleans Band etc ', or HMV's ' Django and his American friends '; examples of a particular instrument or instruments, eg Camden's 'Great jazz brass ' and ' Great jazz reeds '; examples of a particular form, eg Fontana's ' Nothin' but the blues ' and London's ' Ragtime piano roll ': historical factors eg Parlophone's ' Jazz of the twenties ' and ' Jazz in the making '; performance at a concert or festival, eg Fontana's ' The sound of jazz ' or Top Rank's ' Spirituals to swing '. The simplest way of dealing with such collections is to treat them all as anthologies, though the first kind could be arranged by the featured musician. Again, the individual groups would have to be traced via the index.

Despite the snags, this method does bring together a good proportion of the recordings of any group and it is certainly more useful than either of the other methods discussed. For labelling the covers, the first three letters of the group's name will usually be sufficient. When necessary, the numbers of letters will have to be increased, eg Beri and Berr to distinguish Bunny Berigan from Chu Berry. Identical surnames may be distinguished by means of an initial in brackets, eg Hen(F) and Hen(H) for Fletcher and Horace Henderson respectively. Anthologies may be marked with a single A so that they file before everything else. Wherever there is more than one record by a group a method of sub-arrangement will be needed. The simplest method is to number from one onwards as the records are added to the collection, eg anthologies would be marked A1, A2, A3, etc. Tune titles do not provide a feasible means, since even 78s contain two, and album titles of LPs are too erratic to be useful. The method that will recommend itself to systematic collectors is chronological arrangement.

Again, owing to the vagaries of record companies, it is a method that can only be imperfectly applied, but I think it is worth doing. For collections consisting predominantly of LPs the best method is to use the year of recording. As all records were made in the twentieth century, it is only necessary to use two digits. For records containing performances from more than one year, the latest date may be used. Most records will now bear a distinctive mark, eg RCA's Ellington 'In a mellotone' and 'At his very best' will be marked Ell42 and Ell46 respectively. If later additions to the collection require a number already allocated, they can be marked, for example, Ell42/1, Ell42/2 etc. Collections consisting mainly of 78s may be more precisely arranged by month and day if necessary. An alternative for a collection of this kind is the use of session numbers. With the aid of a discography each recording session of a group can be allocated a number. For example, using Rust 1897-1931, Jelly Roll Morton's 1926 piano solo session would be Mor13. Separate 78s from the same session could be numbered, for example, Mor13/1, Mor13/2, etc. As EPs often contain a whole session the method could also be applied to them.

In my own experience the desire to play records of a certain kind is as frequent as the desire to play records by a particular group, and it is obviously a great convenience to be able to quickly select such a batch of records from the collection. Fortunately, there is no conflict here with arrangement by groups. It merely means that instead of a single alphabetical sequence of performers there will be several sequences according to the number of styles to be distinguished.

Classification by style is likely to be controversial and imprecise in any art. This doesn't mean that it is impossible as a practical convenience or that it need be entirely subjective. Of course, any collector is free to follow his own inclination. If he finds that he gets a similar experience from listening to Sidney Bechet, Charlie Parker and Ornette Coleman then he can group them together in his collection. Most listeners, however, will have rather different reactions to these three performers and I believe that a broad consensus of opinion on styles can be found. I am sure that many experienced collectors would prefer to use this more objective method, while for the beginner it is an aid to learning about music and increasing the pleasure of listening. Libraries are well used to the idea of systematic arrangement of materials being based on such consensus. I do not propose to discuss styles in detail but merely to make some suggestions. For those who wish to examine the subject thoroughly I have listed at the end of the chapter some books and articles that may be profitably studied.

There is one precise method of classifying the records, and that is by periods. One could use decades for the divisions or else follow the pattern of the discographies of Rust and Jepsen, referred to in chapter 2. Against the advantage of simplicity we have to offset two disadvantages of the period classification. Styles certainly have a starting point in time but, so far, none of them has a finishing point. This means that each successive period division will contain more variety of styles. Since our objective is to have similar records together, this method is not very successful, except perhaps for the very first period. The second disadvantage is that the work of many performers will be split up into two or more divisions. Armstrong and Ellington, for example, would be spread over the whole lot. This second disadvantage could be overcome by putting all the records of a group in the period of origin. Thus, all the records made under Armstrong's name would be in the 'twenties group and all those of Basie in the 'thirties. This device is used a little in the Rust discographies, but only for performers whose work ended during the following periods. But even if we use it fully there will still be many records in older styles mixed up with the newer. The next step, therefore, would be to keep with the original period all records in styles originating in that period. If we were using the periods provided by the Rust/Jepsen discographies the result would be the tripartite division which everybody uses today in discussing jazz—Traditional, Mainstream and Modern. There is little difficulty in classifying by these three categories and it is about as far as one can go if reasonably well-defined boundaries are required. Many collectors will be satisfied with this.

However, since I can't imagine that I am unique, there will be others who wish to go further. For them I make the following suggestions, which may be considered in the light of the reading referred to earlier. The distinctions I make are not precise and it may be difficult to decide on the right place for some records. On the whole, though, I have found the resulting system both workable and useful—and I think it is as near as one can get to a consensus of opinion.

TRADITIONAL JAZZ

The fundamental distinction between Traditional, Mainstream and Modern must obviously stand: the question is how each of these may be further divided. This can best be answered by examining the characteristics of the period in which each style arose. If we take the period covered by Rust volume I (up to 1931) as the period in which traditional jazz predominated we can detect two main characteristics. (It is important to remember that we are classifying *records*. The relation of what has been preserved to what was played is interesting, but need not concern us now.) The first characteristic is that the vast majority of the recordings are American and that they reflect regional styles. The second is that the recording groups consist of either Negro or white musicians. Mixed bands came later, as did the diffusion of styles, first throughout America as a whole and then throughout the world. Using these two characteristics we may distinguish the following styles:

*1 Negro*

a) New Orleans. I am using this term in the narrowest sense of music made by New Orleans musicians in New Orleans. There are few such records from this period—Piron, Celestin, Dumaine, Morgan, Jones and Collins Astoria Hot Eight, one record by Fate Marable and a handful of vocals. It is a very small sample from which to obtain a general idea of New Orleans style of the time, but at least the first four groups mentioned have a rather different sound from anything recorded elsewhere during the same period and are sufficient to justify this category. The Jones and Collins group are presumably not typical, though I am not aware of any definite evidence that there weren't other similar groups in New Orleans.

b) Chicago Breakdown. I take this term from *The jazz record book*, where it is used to describe the development of New Orleans music in Chicago. I am, however, limiting it to the negro musicians, as a way of distinguishing it from that of the white Chicagoans. This is a fairly large group, its essence consisting of the recordings of Armstrong's Hot Five & Seven, Dodds, Morton, Noone & Oliver. The residue includes Lovie Austin, the Bertrand/Blythe groups, R M Jones, Keppard, Parham, Jabbo Smith, Albert Wynn, Omer Simeon etc.

c) Harlem. The most important effect of this category is to bring together the recordings showing the development of the big bands—Fletcher Henderson, Charlie Johnson, McKinney's Cotton Pickers, etc. The early Ellington also belongs here, but if all his records are to be kept together they are more appropriate in a later section. A similar problem arises with the late Olivers and Mortons. In all cases of this kind the choice has to be made between keeping together all the work of a particular leader or distributing it according to stylistic phases. The other important series of recordings here is that of Clarence Williams, which is a mixture of the bigger band tendency and small groups like the Blue Five and Washboard Band in the style of the Chicago musicians. In addition there are a number of small group recordings by musicians such as Johnny Dunn, Bubber Miley, Thomas Morris and Buddy Christian; and the early work of the Harlem pianists, James P Johnson and Fats Waller.

d) The South-West. This is another class which, like New Orleans, is represented by few recordings. They include the Kansas City bands of Bennie Moten, George Lee and Walter Page; Troy Floyd from San Antonio; and the handful of performances recorded in St Louis by Charlie Creath, Dewey Jackson and Jessie Stone. Until recently this was the least known of the early styles. It has been well treated by Franklin Driggs in *Jazz: new perspectives* . . . , edited by Albert McCarthy, and by Gunther Schuller in *Early jazz*. There are also three LPs available of these territory bands, one on Parlophone and two on the American Historical label.

2 *White*

a) Dixieland. There are rather more examples preserved of the music of white musicians of New Orleans than there are of the negro originators of the style. Between 1924 and 1929 recordings were made by Bayersdorffer, Brownlees Orchestra, De Droit, The Halfway House Orchestra, Hazel, Miller, The New Orleans Owls, The Original Crescent City Jazzers, Papalia and Parenti. The New Orleans groups that recorded in other cities should also be included—The Original Dixieland Jazz Band, the New Orleans Rhythm Kings, Merritt Brunies and the Arcadian Serenaders.

b) The Chicagoans. Another small class. It would have to include such groups as the Wolverines, the early Mannones and the Bucktown Five as well as the more precisely defined Chicago style recordings made under the names of Condon, McKenzie, The Cellar Boys, the Chicago Rhythm Kings, The Jungle Kings and Charles Pierce.

c) White New York. Recordings in this category are far more numerous than any of those preceding. Generally speaking, the criterion for inclusion is the presence of one or more of a small group of musicians—Bix, Trumbauer, Nichols, Mole, Napoleon, Rollini, Dorsey Brothers, Venuti, Lang, Goodman and Teagarden.

There is no white equivalent of the South-West class.

Having provided for the contents of Rust volume I we now have to see what later recordings there are in similar styles. Within any one style the arrangement can be in one alphabetical sequence, or in time periods.

*New Orleans.* This remains to date the easiest class to define, since New Orleans is unique in having retained a style of its own beyond the first period of jazz. Despite its importance, the major record companies have continued to neglect it and most of the recordings we owe to lovers of the music such as Rudi Blesh, William Russell and Grayson Mills. There are no records from the 'thirties, but a reasonable number since then. Only one band, George Lewis's, has recorded regularly, so that this class is a suitable candidate for arrangement by periods. The 'forties are dominated by Bunk Johnson and the American Music label, but there were a number of other important small labels such as Circle, Delta, Good Time Jazz, Jazz Information, Jazz Man, and New Orleans. There is much less from the 'fifties and most of it is included in the ' Music of New Orleans ' series arranged by Samuel Charters for Folkways. So far the 'sixties have produced two important series on Grayson Mills' Icon label and the Riverside ' New Orleans: the Living Legends ', as well as many more recordings on small labels.

*Chicago Breakdown.* Additions to this class will consist of any records continuing or developing the original tradition, whether in Chicago or elsewhere. There are a few such records made in the 'thirties for example, Bechet, Noone, Richard M Jones, The

Harlem Hamfats, Albert Ammons' Rhythm Kings, and the Ladnier/Mezzrow sessions. 1940 saw the issue of the Decca New Orleans Album and since that time the chief recordings in the idiom have been by Armstrong, Bechet, Ory and Wilbur de Paris. Others include groups led by Omer Simeon, Edmond Hall, Albert Nicholas, Mezzrow, Mutt Carey and Punch Miller (the 'forties only—his later recordings are in the New Orleans class). Since these records mainly continue the work of artists who began in the first period, they may be arranged in a single sequence.

*Harlem and the South-West.* These styles merged into the mainstream of Swing in the 'thirties. I don't think there is anything not covered by Rust volume I except a few recreations of Harlem music by Cecil Scott's Washboard Band (Col(E) 33SX1232), Elmer Snowden's Quartet (Riv. RLP 348) and Cliff Jackson's Washboard Wanderers (Prestige/Swingsville 2026).

*Dixieland.* A few recordings in this style were made in the 'thirties under the names of Sharkey Bonano, Wingy Mannone, Paul Mares, The New Orleans Rhythm Kings and Santo Pecora. The distinctive Chicago style is virtually limited to the 'twenties and the White New York style petered out in the early 'thirties with the late recordings of Trumbauer, Venuti and Adrian Rollini. Musicians of all these groups came together in New York and the name Dixieland has since been given to their joint products, which have also included Negro musicians from time to time. Apart from the most famous name of Eddie Condon there are the recordings of Muggsy Spanier, Wild Bill Davison, Bud Freeman, Bobby Hackett, The Bobcats, Yank Lawson, Doc Evans, etc. In addition, of course, there are all the Revivalist bands, starting with Lu Watters in 1941. This class could be arranged in three sections: the original Dixieland style of the 'twenties and 'thirties; the later Dixieland style; and the Revivalists. One might also keep separate those records made by mainstream musicians playing in a loose dixieland pattern, *eg* Roy Eldridge ' Swing goes Dixie ' (Verve V1010).

MAINSTREAM JAZZ: The bulk of Rust volume 2 (1932-1942) consists of the recordings of the big Swing bands and the small groups composed of musicians from them. Many of the small groups are mixed and the negro and white big bands differ only in quality. In the circumstances the only useful division to be made here

139

is between big bands and small bands. After this period the Swing bands, with the exception of Basie and Ellington, virtually disappear, but the great musicians of the 'thirties, such as Roy Eldridge and Coleman Hawkins have continued recording in small groups up to the present. Their work is therefore best kept in one sequence irrespective of date.

MODERN JAZZ: The nearer we get to the present the more difficult it becomes to be certain of categories. The clearest distinction in this period seems to be between the hot and the cool tendencies. Collectors of modern jazz may wish to divide these two groups further. For example, the original Bop of the 'forties can be separated from the later hard-bop and the predominantly white West-Coast School can be kept apart from the Eastern groups. Even finer distinctions have been made in the literature but are not necessarily practicable for arranging records.

As Berendt has pointed out in his *New jazz book,* a new style has appeared in jazz in each decade. The term Modern Jazz still serves not only for the Bop of the 'forties and cool of the 'fifties but also for the latest developments by musicians such as Ornette Coleman and Albert Ayler. Once you have labelled a style Modern it is difficult to find a suitable term for what comes later. *Avant garde* seems the best in use and will serve for the present though I can't imagine what the music of the 'seventies will be called. The flirtations with classical music that have come to be known as Third Stream form a group of their own, and at least one other new hybrid, Indo-Jazz, may be distinguished.

BLUES AND OTHER FORMS RELATED TO JAZZ: The most important form here is, of course, the Blues. This can be a field for specialization as complex as jazz itself. The article by Paul Oliver in Hentoff and McCarthy's *Jazz* suggests a variety of regional styles, but it is doubtful whether they are practicable for classifying records. The classic blues of the 'twenties can certainly be separated from the various forms of folk blues, but as they have close affinities with the early jazz, collectors may prefer to keep these records in the Traditional Group. The piano blues known as boogie-woogie are also susceptible to this alternative treatment. The remainder of Afro-American folk music may be divided into religious and secular, but those with large enough collections will want to use more specific categories, such as work songs and spirituals. Ragtime is in a class by itself and presents no problems. Finally, provision must be made for the jazz-tinged popular music that is likely to find its way into most collections. What precisely belongs this side of the boundary is a matter of judgment. Each collector will have his own views, though I believe that even in this a reasonable consensus of opinion could be established.

## SPECIAL COLLECTIONS

Many collectors specialise in the work of a particular artist such as Bix Beiderbecke or Billie Holiday. If desired, these can be kept together under the artist's name, in chronological or any other suitable order. They may be placed either in the stylistic category to which the artist belongs or in a separate sequence for special collections. This separate sequence may also be used to accommodate works that belong to more than one of the suggested categories, for example, Louis Armstrong's, or are really in a class by themselves, such as Duke Ellington's. Some collectors may prefer to keep solo piano and vocal records apart. This can be done either within the main categories, for example Earl Hines in Mainstream, and Thelonius Monk in modern, or in the special sequence. The jazz of countries other than America is best arranged separately, either in one sequence or by country. In either case they may be subdivided into Traditional, Mainstream, and Modern. Expatriate American musicians are most suitably kept in their appropriate style in the main sequence.

## SUGGESTIONS FOR A CLASSIFICATION OF JAZZ RECORDS

To summarize the foregoing discussion, I offer two suggestions for a classification scheme; the first gives precedence to stylistic categories, the second subordinates them to period divisions. Alternatives are also suggested for specific divisions and many other variations are possible.

Letters have been used in preference to numbers for the notation as they produce shorter symbols. The single letters have been allocated to sections likely to include the most records. Further detail can be added, if and where required, by using further letters for subdivision; and a completely different notation can be used if anyone wishes to incorporate this outline in a classification for a collection of wider scope.

| A | *Collections* |
|------|------|
| AB | Histories |
| AC | Miscellaneous anthologies |
| AD | Festivals and concerts—' live ' recordings |
| AF | Collections by instrument (may be arranged as class **P** of the jazz literature classification; see chapter 3) |
| AG | Collections by musician |

| B | *Traditional (collections)* |
|------|------|
| BB | Classic blues singers (alternative XC) |
| BC | Boogie-Woogie (alternative XD) |
| C | New Orleans |
| CB | 'Twenties |
| CC | 'Forties |
| CD | 'Fifties |
| CF | 'Sixties |
| D | Chicago breakdown |
| DB | 'Twenties and 'Thirties |
| DC | 'Forties onwards |
| DF | South-West |
| DH | Harlem |
| F | Dixieland |
| FB | 'Twenties and 'Thirties |
| FC | 'Forties onwards—originators of the style |
| FD | Revivalists |
| FF | Swing goes Dixie |
| FM | Chicagoans |
| G | White New York |

| J | *Mainstream (collections)* |
|------|------|
| JB | Singers |
| JC | Pianists |
| K | Small groups |
| L | Big bands |

| M | *Modern (collections)* |
|------|------|
| MB | Singers |

| MC | Pianists |
|----|----------|
| N  | Bop |
| P  | Cool |

| R | *Avant garde* |
|---|---------------|

| T  | *Hybrids* |
|----|-----------|
| TB | Afro-Cuban |
| TC | Third Stream |
| TD | Indo-Jazz |

| TP | *Jazz and Poetry* |
|----|-------------------|

| V | *Jazz of countries other than USA* |
|---|-------------------------------------|

May be divided alphabetically by country and then by style, *eg* VFB = French traditional jazz.

| W  | *Afro-American folk music (collections)* |
|----|------------------------------------------|
| WB | Religious (spirituals, etc) |
| WC | Secular (worksongs, etc) |

| X  | *Blues (collections)* |
|----|-----------------------|
| XB | Country |
| XC | Classic (alternative BB) |
| XD | Boogie-Woogie (alternative BC) |
| XF | City |
| XG | Rhythm and Blues |
| XH | Soul |

| Y | *Ragtime* |
|---|-----------|

| Z | *Popular Music* |
|---|-----------------|

SUGGESTION (2) FOR A CLASSIFICATION OF JAZZ RECORDS—EMPHASIZING PERIODS

| A  | *Collections* |
|----|---------------|
| AB | Histories |
| AC | Miscellaneous |
| AD | Festivals and Concerts |
| AF | Collections by Instrument (may be arranged as class P of the jazz literature classification—see chapter 3) |
| AG | Collections by Musician |

| | | | |
|------|----------------------------------------------|-------------|-----|
| AW   | *Early Jazz* ('twenties and early 'thirties). Collections | | |
| AX   | Classic Blues Singers ⎫ | | ⎧ ZG |
| AY   | Boogie-Woogie ⎬ Alternative | | ⎨ ZH |
| AZ   | Ragtime ⎭ | | ⎩ ZR |
| B    | New Orleans | | |
| C    | Chicago Breakdown | | |
| CB   | South West | | |
| CC   | Harlem | | |
| D    | Dixieland | | |
| DB   | Chicagoans | | |
| F    | New York (White) | | |

| | |
|------|------------------------------------------------|
| G    | *Swing period* (Early 30s to early 40s). Collections |
| GB   | Singers |
| GC   | Pianists |
| H    | Small groups |
| J    | Big bands |

| | |
|------|------------------------------------------------|
| K    | *Modern period* (early 'forties to present). Collections |

| | |
|------|------------------------------------------------|
| L    | New Orleans |
| LB   | 'Forties |
| LC   | 'Fifties |
| LD   | 'Sixties |

| | |
|------|------------------------------------------------|
| M    | Chicago Breakdown |

| | |
|------|------------------------------------------------|
| N    | Dixieland |
| NB   | Originators and Chicago musicians continuing in this style |
| NC   | Revivalists |
| ND   | Swing goes Dixie |

| | |
|------|------------------------------------------------|
| P    | Mainstream |
| PB   | Singers |
| PC   | Pianists |
| Q    | Small groups |
| QB   | Big bands |

| R | Modern | |
|---|---|---|
| RB | Singers | |
| RC | Pianists | |
| S | Bop, Hard bop | } Alternative S 'Forties |
| T | Cool, Progressive | } T 'Fifties and 'Sixties |
| V | Avant garde | |

| X | *Hybrids* |
|---|---|
| XB | Afro-Cuban |
| XC | Third Stream |
| XD | Indo-Jazz |

| XP | *Jazz and poetry* |
|---|---|

| Y | *Jazz of countries other than USA* |
|---|---|

May be divided alphabetically by country, *eg* YF = French jazz

May be further divided by style as K—X, *eg* YFR = French Modern jazz

| Z | *Afro American folk-music* |
|---|---|
| ZB | Religious (Spirituals, etc) |
| ZC | Secular (Worksongs, etc) |
| ZD | Blues |
| ZF | Country |
| ZG | Classic (alternative AX) |
| ZH | Boogie-Woogie (alternative AY) |
| ZJ | City |
| ZK | Rhythm and Blues |
| ZL | Soul |

| ZR | *Ragtime* (Alternative AZ) |
|---|---|

| ZS | *Popular music* |
|---|---|

INDEXING THE RECORDS

If records are arranged by names or styles the collection is partially self-indexing: anyone whose requirement is merely to find a record by a given band will be able to manage without an index (as long as he can remember which bands are not in their right place for the reasons discussed). In this case it is not even necessary to label the records. Even the arrangement by styles can be quickly memorized. Many collectors, however, will want at least an index of musicians and tunes.

The form of the index must be flexible, and this means either cards or loose-leaf books. Size will depend on how much information each entry has to carry. I shall mainly be concerned with a very full indexing method based on the classified arrangement of the records. Anyone can then take as much or as little as he needs. To give some idea of the range of possibilities, however, I begin with the simplest form possible.

Let us assume that the records are also arranged in the simplest way, by accession numbers, and that the first record added to the collection is ' I cried for you ' and ' I'll get by ' by Teddy Wilson and his orchestra on a 78 disc. Index entries could then be made as follows:

1) Musician's index

| HODGES, Johnny | HOLIDAY, Billie |
|---|---|
| (78)1 | (78)1 |

2) Tune index

| I CRIED FOR YOU | I'LL GET BY |
|---|---|
| Teddy Wilson & his Orchestra (78)1 | Teddy Wilson & his Orchestra (78)1 |

ETC

For a collection containing all sizes of records the musicians' index may be partitioned vertically, for example:

| HODGES, Johnny | | | |
|---|---|---|---|
| 78 | 7 | 10 | 12 |
| 1, 3, 9 21, 24 | 2, 3 | | 4, 7, 11 |

If economy of stationery is sought, a smaller card may be used for the tune index. Obviously, most entries for musicians will contain more entries than those for tunes. The alternative is to use the smallest convenient size for everything and add extra cards for musicians that need them.

These examples demonstrate that the minimum requirement is an entry which identifies each item sought, with a reference to the record identification number. In the case of musicians the name is sufficient, in the case of tunes the title and name of performer(s) are necessary.

After this brief examination of elementary principles one can now turn to the full range of indexing possibilities.

MAIN INDEX

From now on I shall assume that the records are arranged by the classified method previously described, and that the index is to provide for a variety of approaches. It is better to keep a separate sequence of cards for each aspect indexed. Arrangement of the cards is simpler this way, and it also means that different treatment can be accorded the various sequences if desired—both as to size and content of entries.

The reasons for having a main sequence are as follows:

1) A good index will show the full resources of the collection as well as indicate the whereabouts of individual items. The main sequence can be made to do this both by its method of arrangement and by the amount of detail in each entry.

2) Even if the records are arranged in a systematic way they do not by themselves reveal very much. One record can hardly be distinguished from another until it is taken out of position, and the spines are too narrow to clearly display information. Books are far more helpful in this respect.

3) Even if the owner has a good idea of the contents of his collection, the index is the only effective way of showing anyone else what it contains. Many collectors will want to do this; all libraries have to.

THE UNIT OF ENTRY AND ARRANGEMENT IN THE MAIN INDEX

It is important to remember that our ultimate concern is with the music in the grooves, and not with the records as physical objects. We have already seen that the heterogeneous nature of many issues is a definite hindrance to the completely systematic arrangement of the records themselves, but in the index we can overcome this difficulty. It is possible, of course, to make each

147

entry in the main index represent a record, but this is merely repeating the unsatisfactory grouping of performances. What we need in the main index is a *natural* unit of entry. In classical music this would be a single work of a given composer—a symphony, a quintet or a song. In jazz, the homogeneous unit is not the single theme but the recording session, whether it consists of one or a dozen performances.

With this basis it is possible to achieve what I consider to be the most effective type of main index—a complete list of the performances in the collection arranged primarily by styles, within each style by alphabetical order of performing units, and within each performing unit by chronological order of recording sessions. Such an index not only reveals the scope of the collection in a way that records themselves cannot, but also represents the perfect order that the records only partially achieve.

The effect can be judged by scanning a discography or guide to jazz records with a similar method of arrangement. The best example is *The jazz record book* by Charles Edward Smith and others. *Hot discography*, in all its editions, has a classified form, though the arrangement here is rather more idiosyncratic. Despite the superiority in detail and accuracy of later discographies, I still find *Hot discography* the most fascinating, simply because it does bring similar recordings together.

HEADINGS IN THE MAIN INDEX

The heading for each entry should obviously be the name of the recording group or soloist. We have already seen, in examining methods of arranging records, that difficulties arise through the same band recording under different names and through variations in record labels. The second of these can be overcome by using discographies rather than records to establish headings, and the first by using a standard name. I have mentioned that *Jazz directory* uses this principle. *Hot discography* is also helpful, and Orin Blackstone's *Index to jazz*, though it doesn't arrange by standard headings, has cross-references which make it easy to trace the various names of a group. Headings of this kind may be written as follows:

RUSSELL, Luis
(Henry Allen jr and his New York Orchestra)

Similarly, for those records collected on account of a particular musician one may have a heading such as:

BEIDERBECKE, Bix
(Paul Whiteman and his orchestra)

CONTENTS OF THE MAIN ENTRY

The fullest possible entry would include place and date of recording, matrix and take number, title, record number, personnel and order of solos, bibliographical details of reviews or analyses of the recording, and the identification mark for locating the record in the collection. If the collector has a range of discographies he may decide that it is not worthwhile putting full details in his own index. Writing out personnels, particularly, is very time consuming. The basic entry may then be reduced to date of recording (for chronological arrangement of sessions), titles, take numbers if appropriate (*ie* where there was more than one take of any title), and record location mark. Personnels are usually given on modern record covers and this is certainly the most convenient place to have them. However, they are not always accurate, and should be checked with the discographies. Where there are errors they may be noted on the index card. If the discographies differ from each other this also should be noted. It is not easy to establish who is right in such cases, but the information may be available in the discographical columns of jazz magazines or in articles on particular musicians. Order of solos is obviously useful information wherever there is more than one performer on a particular instrument. They are not given in the general discographies, but some special studies do include them, for example *King Joe Oliver* by Allen and Rust, and *Duke Ellington: his life and music,* edited by Peter Gammond. Here again, articles on particular musicians may be useful, and reference books such as Panassié's *Dictionary of jazz.* Details of reviews form an optional item which some collectors may like to add.

We can now see what a main entry constructed on these lines would be like. The following entry would be filed firstly by the classification mark, meaning Harlem style, secondly by the standard name, and thirdly by the date of the session. The rest of the information shows that there are two different versions of each of the titles, in the collection, one set on a 78 record, the other on

a 7 inch microgroove. The reverse side of the card may be used
for any further information, on personnel, solos, etc.

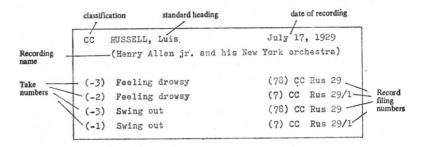

As an alternative to writing on the index card only those titles
already acquired, one could start with a complete list of titles in
the order that they were recorded and fill in the record filing
numbers as they were added to the collection. This is probably
the most efficient method for those artists for whom one hopes
eventually to compile a complete collection.

SECONDARY INDEXES

The main index refers to the records by means of their identification marks. Secondary indexes may refer either to the records or
to the main index, or to both. Two indexes of this kind are required, one for musicians, and one for titles.

1) *Index of musicians*

The main index systematically arranges the information about
recording sessions and contains the fullest details. The index of
musicians is technically a secondary index, since it is constructed
from the main index and refers to it. But the essence of jazz is in
the individuality of its performers. No collection is adequately
indexed without a guide to the records on which each musician
plays.

For smaller collections it may be adequate to refer from the
musicians' index merely to the records. For large collections it is
better to have in addition a reference to the main index so that
particular performances can be selected. The two kinds of reference may be separately recorded on the front and back of the
index card. If the musician's name is at the left of the top line,
the instrument on which he performs may be written at the

right. The following example shows how the index card for Henry Allen would refer to the main index entry above and to the related records.

| ALLEN, Henry | Trumpet |
| CC Luis Russell | 17/7/29 |

Front of card, referring to main index entry.

| 78 rpm | 7 | 10 | 12 |
|---|---|---|---|
| CC Rus 29 | CC Rus 29/1 | | |

Back of card, referring to record filing numbers.

If a musician occasionally plays another instrument in addition to his regular one, this may be indicated as follows:

| ALLEN, Henry | Vocal[1] | Trumpet |

In the entries on this card it will be understood that trumpet is played in every case, but that vocals occur only on those with the superior index number one attached.

For musicians who regularly play two or more instruments it will be necessary to provide an index number for each, *eg*

| BECHET, Sidney | Clarinet[2] | Soprano[1] |

2) *Index of theme titles*

The themes used for improvisation in jazz are of secondary importance to the musicians performing. However, they are not without interest, and many collectors have favourite themes and enjoy comparing different treatments. Entries in this index would preferably include the following items: title, composer, lyric writer (if any), performing group, record filing number, *eg*

| IT SHOULD BE YOU | Henry Allen | |
| *(title)* | *(composer)* | *(lyric writer)* |
| Luis Russell | (7) CC Rus 29 | |
| *(performing group)* | *(record filing number)* | |

151

There are two other indexes a collector may wish to compile. I call them tertiary indexes since they refer neither to the main index nor the record themselves, but to the secondary indexes. The first is an index of composers, which refers to the index of theme titles, *eg*

> ALLEN, Henry
>
> Biffly Blues
>
> It should be you

The second is an index of instruments, which refers to the musicians index, *eg*

> TRUMPET and CORNET
>
> Allen, Ed
>
> Allen, Henry

It is possible to combine this index with the musicians index. Instead of one alphabetical sequence of names there would be a separate sequence for each instrument. For performers on more than one instrument it would be necessary to have a card in each place with a cross-reference from each, *eg*

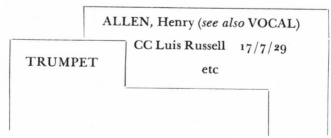

> ALLEN, Henry (*see also* VOCAL)
>
> TRUMPET    CC Luis Russell  17/7/29
>
> etc

## OTHER INDEXES

It would be possible to make further indexes using the characteristics of place, date or instrumentation. They are more likely to be required by those carrying out research than by the 'passive' collector. Punched cards are an ideal medium for such needs. A simple introduction to their use will be found in *A guide to personal indexes* by A C Foskett.

READINGS FOR CHAPTER FOUR
1 *Storage, arrangement and indexing of records*
Angel, R G: ' BBC Gramophone Library cataloguing practice '. Pp 53-69 in Currall, H F (*ed*): *Gramophone record libraries*. Crosby Lockwood, 1963.

Bryant, E T: 'Indexing gramophone records'. *The indexer*, Spring, 1961, pp 90-94.

Bryant, E T: *Music librarianship*. Clarke, 1959.

Foskett, A C: *A guide to personal indexes*. Bingley, 1967.

Pickett, A G & Lemcoe, M M: *Preservation and storage of sound recordings*. Washington, Library of Congress, 1959.

2 *Classification of jazz styles & Afro-American forms*
Berendt, E: *The new jazz book*. New York, Hill and Wang, 1962 (chapter 1).

Borneman, E: *A critic looks at jazz*. Jazz Music Books, 1946.

Dankworth, A: *Jazz: an introduction to its musical basis*. Oxford University Press, 1968 (Part II).

Gammond, P (*ed*): *The Decca book of jazz*. Muller, 1958.

Hodeir, A: *Jazz: its evolution & essence*. Secker & Warburg, 1956 (chapter 2).

Keepnews, O: ' Dixieland '. Pp 57-8 in Williams, M T (*ed*): *The art of jazz*. Cassell, 1959.

Keil, C: *Urban blues*. University of Chicago Press, 1966 (Appendix C).

Lambert, G E: ' Reflections on jazz history and the Chicagoans'. *Jazz monthly*, August 1958, pp 6-9; September 1958, pp 9-11. (Reply by T Standish: ' Reflections in a dusty mirror '. *Jazz monthly*, December 1958, pp 25-27.)

McCarthy, A (*ed*): *Jazz on record*. Hanover Books, 1968 (pp 318-393, esp the various sections on blues by Paul Oliver).

Newton, F: *The jazz scene*. Penguin, 1961 (chapter 6).

Oliver, P: ' Blues to drive the blues away '. Pp 85-103 in Hentoff, N & McCarthy, A (*eds*): *Jazz: new perspectives* . . . Cassell, 1959.

Oliver, P: *Screening the blues*. Cassell, 1968 (pp 182-185).

Ostransky, L: *The anatomy of jazz*. Seattle, University of Washington Press, 1960.

# Index

This index includes all authors and titles mentioned in the text, but not those that are included only in the reading lists.

Aasland, Benny, 50
Accession numbers, 131-132
African elements, 65
Afro-American music, 30, 49, 64, 76, 78, 140-141
Allen, Henry, 32, 45
Allen, Richard, 17, 46
Allen, Walter, 21, 50, 149
Alphabetical indexes, 73-74
*American jazz music*, 64
American Music (records), 17, 138
Ammons, Albert, 139
*Anatomy of bibliomania, The*, 15
'Anatomy of improvisation, The ', 62
*Anatomy of jazz, The*, 33, 65
Ansermet, Ernest, 66
Anthologies, Record: indexing, 133
Antiquarian interests, 18, 20-21, 23
*Anything goes: The world of popular music*, 24
*Appeal of jazz, The*, 56
Arcadian Serenaders, 138
Archive of Folk-song, 46
Armagnac, Percy, 47
Armstrong, Lil, 63
Armstrong, Louis, 25, 63, 66, 135, 137, 139, 141
Arrangement
  books and indexes, 73-74, 105-122
  discographies, 52-53
  record indexes, 148
  records, 130-145
Art collecting, 11
Art jazz, 37-38
*Art of happiness, The*, 14
*Art of jazz, The*, 62
Association for Recorded Sound Collections, 47

Austin, Lovie, 137
Austin, William, 58
Autobiography: musicians, 66, 70
Avant garde jazz, 38, 140
Ayler, Albert, 140

*B.G.—off the record*, 50
Bad books on jazz, 67
' Ballad of Reading Gaol ', 33-34
Balliett, Whitney, 28, 62
Bands: collecting, 38
Barazetta, Giuseppe, 51
Barker, Danny, 46
Basie, Count, 16, 66, 135, 140
Bayersdorffer, Johnny, 137
Bechet, Sidney, 26, 48, 66, 134, 138, 139
Beiderbecke, Bix, 26, 67, 138
Berendt, Joachim, 59, 65, 140
Bernstein, Leonard, 66
Bertrand, Jimmy, 137
Bibliographies, 57-58, 59
*Bibliography of jazz, A*, 57, 75
*Big bands, The*, 58
Bio-discographies, 50, 54
Biography: musicians, 66-67, 70
*Birth of the blues, The*, 45
' Bix Beiderbecke legend, The ', 26
*Black magic*, 59
*Black music*, 38
Blackstone, Orin, 17, 49, 51, 148
Bland, Bobby, 34
Blesh, Rudi, 64, 65, 67, 138
Blues, 30-31, 64, 140
*Blues and gospel records 1902-1942*, 49, 50
*Blues people*, 64
*Blues research*, 51

Blythe, Jimmy, 137
Bobcats, 139
Bonano, Sharkey, 139
Book collecting, 15, 55-56
*Book of jazz, The,* 62
Bop, 38, 140
*Born with the blues,* 64
Borneman, Ernest, 27
Bradford, Perry, 64
*Brandy of the damned, The,* 15
*British Catalogue of Music classification,* 76
British Institute of Jazz Studies, 46
British Institute of Recorded Sound, 16
Brownlees Orchestra, 137
Brunies, Merritt, 138
Brunn, Ho, 67
Bruyninchx, Walter, 50
Bucktown Five, 138
*Bugles for Beiderbecke,* 67

' Careless love ', 38
Carew, Thomas, 35
Carey, Dave, 49, 51, 132
Carey, Mutt, 139
Carmichael, Hoagy, 36
Carter, John, 11
Categories
  jazz subjects, 77
  jazz writing, 61
*Cathay,* 17
Celestin, Oscar, 32, 136
Cellar Boys, 138
Center (records), 32
Cerulli, Dom, 62, 67
Chapman, R W 12, 17
Charters, Samuel, 32, 58, 63, 64, 74, 138
Cherrington, G, 50
' Chicago: the living legends ', 31
Chicago Breakdown, 136-137, 138-139
Chicago Rhythm Kings, 138
Chicago South Side jazz, 31
Chicagoans, 138, 139
Christian, Buddy, 137
Chronicles, 52, 64
Chronological
  arrangement of records, 133-134, 135
  order of tracks on reissues, 25
Circle (records), 138
Clark, *Sir* Kenneth, 9, 10

Clarke, G F Gray, 16
Classics of jazz, 29-30
Classification
  Afro-American music, 78, 140-141
  books, 73
  element in collecting, 13, 20, 22
  indexes, 73-74, 76-79
  jazz styles, 51, 134-141
  records, 134-145
Classification schemes
  literature of jazz, 80-93
  records, 141-145
Coates, E J, 76
Cobb, Junie, 31
Cole, Cozy, 18
Coleman, Ornette, 134, 140
' Coleman Hawkins: a documentary ', 63
Collecting and collectors, 9-43
  aids, 44-72
  books and records, 15-17
  first editions, 17-21
  jazz, 21-40
*Collector's jazz, The,* 52
Columbia Record Company, 17, 53
*Columbia 13/14000—D series,* 47
Commercialism: record production, 24
Composer index, 152
Concert halls, 45
Condon, Eddie, 138, 139
Connor, Donald, 50
Coover, J B, 29
*Count Basie and his Orchestra,* 66
Courlander, H, 64
Creath, Charlie, 137
Criticism: musicians, 66-67, 70

Dachs, David, 24
Dance, Stanley, 58
Dance music, 31
Dancehalls, 45
Dankworth, Avril, 65
Davis, John, 16
Davison, Wild Bill, 26, 139
De Bury, Richard, 13
De Droit, Johnny, 137
De Paris, Wilbur, 139
Dealers: jazz records, 39
Decca Record Company, 53
Delaunay, Charles, 48, 51
Delta (records), 138
Depth indexing, 74

156

*Deutsche 78er Discographie, Die,* 50
Dexter, Dave, 67
*Dictionary of jazz,* 58, 149
*Dinosaurs in the morning,* 28
Discographies, 38
  general, 48-50, 53-54
  individual, 50, 54-55
  national, 50-51, 54
Discography, 48-55
Dixieland, 137-138, 139
Dixieland Hall, 45
Dixon, R M W, 49, 50
Dodds, Johnny, 31, 39-40, 137
Dominique, Natty, 31
Dorsey, Jimmy and Tommy, 138
*Downbeat,* 62, 63
Driggs, Franklin, 17, 137
*Duke Ellington: his life and music,*
  50, 67, 149
Dumaine, Louis, 32, 136
Dunn, Johnny, 137

*Early jazz: its roots and musical de-*
  *velopment,* 65, 137
Echo in records, 18
' Editing ' records, 18
Eldridge, Roy, 139, 140
Elements of jazz, 77
Ellington, Duke
  books on, 50, 67, 149
  indexing, 75, 79, 119-121
  music, 30, 37, 38
  records arrangement, 135, 137, 140,
    141
Ellison, Ralph, 62
*Encyclopedia of jazz, The* 58
Encyclopedias, 58, 60-61
*Enjoy jazz,* 61
Entertainment jazz, 32-37
Enthusiasm for jazz, 56-57
Esquire's yearbooks, 62
Essays on jazz, 62, 68
*Essays on jazz,* 66
*Eureka,* 32
European music and jazz, 66
Evans, Doc, 139
' Every evening ', 36-37

Fans and collectors, 21-22, 39
Farrell, Jack W, 67
Feather, Leonard, 58, 62
' Feeling is gone, The ', 34-35
Festivals, 45

Films, 45
Finkelstein, Sidney, 33, 65
First editions
  books, 17
  records, 17-21, 23
Fitzgerald, Ella, 35
' Five feet of soul ', 33
Floyd, Troy, 137
Folk music, 30-32
Folkways (records), 138
' For Sidney Bechet ', 48
Ford Foundation, 46
Foskett, A C, 152
*Four lives in the bebop business,* 64
Fox, Charles, 26, 30, 31, 62
Freeman, Bud, 139
Functional jazz, 30-32

GHB (records), 32
Gammond, Peter, 50, 67, 149
Garlick, G, 67
Gennett (records), 16
*Giants of jazz,* 67
*Glimpse at the past, A,* 16, 47
Godrich, John, 49, 50
Goffin, Robert, 56
*Golden age recorded, The,* 20
Good Time Jazz (records), 138
Goodman, Benny, 50, 66, 138
Gospel songs, 30
Grauer, Bill, 21, 59
Graves, Robert, 21
' Great music revival, The ', 19
' Great private collections, The ', 9
Green, Benny, 35, 66
Grossman, William L, 67
Grove, Thurman and Mary, 27-28
*Guide to long play jazz records,* 52
*Guide to personal indexes,* 152

HRS (records), 17
Hackett, Bobby, 33, 139
Halfway House Dance orchestra, 137
Hall, David, 47
Hall, Edmond, 139
Hall, Jim, 18
Hammond, John, 16, 17, 27
*Handbook of jazz, A,* 59
Handy, Captain John, 28
Harlem Hamfats, 139
Harlem jazz, 137, 139
Harris, H Meunier, 57
Harris, Rex, 52

Harris, Sheldon, 46
Haselgrove, J R, 57
Hawkins, Coleman, 63, 140
Hayakawa, S I, 33
Hazel, Monk, 137
Headings: record index, 148-149
*Hear me talkin' to ya, The*, 63
*Heart of jazz, The*, 67
Henderson, Fletcher, 132, 137
Hentoff, Nat, 59, 63, 64, 66, 140
Hines, Earl, 36
Histories of jazz, 63-64, 68-69
History of jazz collecting, 26-28
Hobson, Wilder, 27, 64
Hodeir, André, 24, 65, 67
Holiday, Billie, 16, 35-36, 66
Horricks, Raymond, 64, 66, 67
*Hot discography*, 48, 51, 148
*Hot jazz*, 56, 65
Hughes, Langston, 59
Hughes, Ted, 36
*Hugues Panassié discusses 144 hot jazz records*, 53
Humour, 33
Hurst, P G, 20

' I cried for you ', 34-35
' I guess I'll have to change my plan ', 33
*I like jazz*, 61
Icon (records), 32, 138
Ignorance of jazz, 56, 67
Illustrations, 59, 60
*Index to jazz*, 49, 51, 148
Indexing
  books, 73-76
  periodicals, 74-75, 111-128
  records, 130-131, 145-152
Indo-jazz, 140
Institute of Jazz Studies, 46
Institutions for jazz, 44-47
Instruments
  classification, 77
  index, 152
International Association of Jazz Record Collectors, 46-47

*Jack Teagarden's music*, 50
Jackson, Cliff, 139
Jackson, Dewey, 137
Jackson, Holbrook, 15
James, Burnett, 22, 66
James, William, 9

Janis, Harriet, 64
' Japanese sandman ', 28
*Jazz: a history*, 65
*Jazz: a history of the New York scene*, 32, 64, 74
*Jazz: a people's music*, 33, 65
*Jazz: an introduction to its musical basis*, 65
*Jazz: hot and hybrid*, 65
*Jazz: its evolution and essence*, 24, 65, 67
*Jazz: New Orleans 1885-1963*, 32, 58
*Jazz: new perspectives on the history*, 64, 137, 140
*Jazz and pop*, 63
' Jazz and the collector ', 27-28
*Jazz and the white Americans*, 64
*Jazz cataclysm, The*, 64
*Jazz catalogue*, 50, 57, 74-75
Jazz clubs, 45
Jazz Crusade (records), 32
' Jazz cult, The ', 27
*Jazz directory*, 49, 51, 132, 148
*Jazz discography, 1958*, 49
*Jazz era: the forties*, 58
*Jazz in little Belgium*, 51
*Jazz in perspective* (Fox), 62
*Jazz in perspective* (Lang), 64
*Jazz inciso in Italia*, 51
Jazz Information (records), 17, 138
*Jazz journal*, 51, 63
*Jazz—kalender*, 59
*Jazz life, The*, 64
*Jazz makers, The*, 66
Jazz Man (records), 138
*Jazz masters*, 66
*Jazz monthly*, 51, 58, 63
*Jazz on a summer's day*, 45
*Jazz on LPs*, 53
*Jazz on record*, 52
*Jazz on 78s*, 53
*Jazz panorama*, 62
*Jazz record book*, 52, 136, 148
*Jazz records A-Z*, 49, 50, 51, 135-140 passim
*Jazz report*, 26, 63
*Jazz scene, The*, 21, 62, 64
*Jazz story, The*, 67
*Jazz street*, 59
*Jazz studies*, 46
*Jazz word, The*, 62, 67
*Jazzfinder*, 62
*Jazzmen*, 27, 64

Jazzology (records), 32
*Jazzways, 62*
Jefferson, Blind Lemon, 30
Jepsen, Jorgen Grunnet, 49, 50, 51, 135
Johnson, Bunk, 33, 138
Johnson, Charlie, 137
Johnson, James P, 137
Jones, Le Roi, 38, 64
Jones, Richard M, 137, 138
Jones, Spike, 33
Jones and Collins Astoria Hot Eight, 32, 136
Jungle Kings, 138
Junkshopping, 27
*Just jazz, 62*

Keepnews, Orrin, 59
Keil, Charles, 34
Keller, Hans, 15
Kendziora, Carl, 47
Kennington, D, 57
Keppard, Freddie, 137
Kid Thomas-George Lewis Ragtime Stompers, 26
King Jazz (records), 26
*King Joe Oliver, 50, 149*
*Kingdom of swing, The, 66*
*Kings of jazz, 66*
*Know about jazz, 61*
Kramer, Eugene, 18
Kunstadt, Len, 32, 64, 74

La Rocca, Nick, 46
Ladnier, Tommy, 139
*Lady sings the blues, 66*
Lambert, Constant, 66
Lang, Eddie, 138
Lang, Iain, 64
Lange, Horst, 50
Larkin, Philip, 38, 48
' Last trip up the river ', 64
Lawrence, D H, 35
Lawson, Yank, 139
Lee, George, 137
' Legend of Willie " The Lion " Smith, The ', 63
' Legendary Buster Smith, The ', 31
Leonard, Neil, 64
Lewis, George, 26, 32, 138
Libraries,
    indexing policy, 75-76
    jazz collecting policy, 29, 39

Library of Congress, 46
Lindsay, Martin, 62
Lipskin, Mike, 19
*Literature of jazz, The, 57*
' Live ' performances of jazz, 22, 44
*Living forwards, 22*
*Lock, stock and barrel, 9*
Locker-Lampson, Frederick, 13
Lomax, Alan, 46, 63
Lomax, John, 46
London (records), 53
Longstreet, Stephen, 67
' Louis Armstrong 1925-1929 ', 25

McCarthy, Albert, 48, 49, 51, 132, 137, 140
McCuen, Brad, 19
McDougall, William, 9
McKenzie, Red, 138
McKinney's Cotton Pickers, 137
McRae, Barry, 64
' Magpies ', 10
Mahogany Hall, 46
Mahony, Dan, 47
Main index : records, 147-150
Mainstream jazz, 16, 139-140
' Mandy is Two ', 36
Mannone, Wingy, 138, 139
Marable, Fate, 136
Mares, Paul, 139
Massagli, L, 50
*Matrix, 51*
Media for jazz, 44-45
Mellers, Wilfrid, 30, 66
Melodeon (records), 17
*Melody maker, 63*
Meltzer, Milton, 59
Mendl, R W S, 56
Menuhin, Yehudi, 15
Merriam, Alan, 57, 58, 75
*Metronome, 62, 63*
Mezzrow, Milton, 26, 66, 139
Miley, Bubber, 137
Miller, Glenn, 37
Miller, Johnny, 137
Miller, Punch, 139
Mills, Grayson, 138
Modern jazz, 37-38, 140
*Modern jazz: developments since 1939, 64*
Mole, Miff, 138
Mono (records), 32
Montgomery, Wes, 18
Morgan, Alun, 64

Morgan, Sam, 32, 136
Morgenstern, Dan, 45
Morris, Thomas, 137
Morton, Jelly Roll, 37, 38, 63, 137
Moten, Bennie, 137
*Mr Jelly Roll*, 63
*Music Ho!*, 66
*Music in a new found land*, 30, 66
*Music in the 20th century*, 58
*Music index*, 74
' Music of New Orleans ', 63, 138
Musical analysis, 65-66, 69
Musicians
    arrangement of records, 132-134
    classification, 77
    criticism, 66-67, 70
    index, 150-151, 152
    specialization in collecting, 38
' Muskrat ramble ', 33

Napoleon, Phil, 138
National discographies, 50-51, 54
Negro folk music, 30-31, 32, 36
*Negro folk music, USA*, 64
Negro styles, 136-137, 138-139
*New jazz book, The*, 65, 140
New Orleans (City), 44
New Orleans (records), 17, 138
' New Orleans: the living legends ',
    32, 138
New Orleans Archive, 46
New Orleans jazz
    classification, 136, 138
    collecting, 31-32
    neglect by record companies, 16
    youthfulness, 21
*New Orleans jazz: a family album*,
    32, 58, 59
New Orleans Jazz Club, 32
New Orleans Jazz Museum, 32, 46
New Orleans Owls, 137
New Orleans Rhythm Kings, 138, 139
New York City, 64
New York jazz, 138, 139
Newport Jazz Festival 1958, 45
Newton, Francis, 21, 62, 64
Nicholas, Albert, 139
Nichols, Red, 37, 138
Nightclubs, 45
Noone, Jimmie, 36-37, 137, 138

Oliver, King, 45, 50, 137, 149
Oral history, 46

Original Crescent City Jazzers, 137
Original Dixieland Jazz Band, 46,
    138
' Origins of jazz ', 53
Ory, Kid, 139
Osgood, H O, 56
Ostransky, Leroy, 33, 65, 66
*Our language and our world*, 33
*Oxford companion to music*, 56

Page, Walter, 137
Panassié, Hugues, 53, 56, 58, 65, 149
Papalia, Russ, 137
Paramount (records), 47
Parenti, Tony, 26, 137
Parham, Tiny, 137
*Paris blues*, 45
Parker, Charlie, 26, 134
Partisan writing, 67
Pathological collecting, 10
Pearl (records), 32
Pecora, Santo, 139
' Perfect dance and race catalogue ',
    47
Periodicals, 62-63
Pernet, Robert, 51
Personnels, 149
' Piano ', 35
*Pictorial history of jazz, A*, 59
Pierce, Charles, 138
' Pirate ' record companies, 20
Piron, Armand, 136
Planning collections, 39-40
Poetry London's yearbooks, 62
Popular music, 33-37
    guides and indexes, 58-59, 60-61
' Popular songs vs the facts of life ',
    33
Pound, Ezra, 17
Powys, John Cowper, 14
Preservation
    records, 16
    the past, 11-13
Preservation Hall, 45
*Preservation Hall portraits*, 59
Priestley, J B, 25
Primers of jazz, 61-62, 68
Progressive jazz, 38
Pseudonyms, 51
*Psychological abstracts*, 9
Psychology
    collecting, 9-11
    record length, 28-29
Punched cards, 152

160

RCA Victor, 18-19, 20, 53
*RSVP*, 26, 63
Race records, 31
Ragtime, 64
Ramsey, Frederic, 52, 64
*Readers' guide to books on jazz*, 57
*Really the blues*, 66
*Record changer, The*, 20, 63
*Record research*, 26, 51
*Recorded jazz: a critical guide*, 52
Recording companies, 47
    major, 16-17, 20
    small, 16-17, 25
    *see also* names of specific labels
' Recording limits and blues form ',
    28
Recording names, 132
Records
    arrangement, 130-145
    as physical objects, 10-11, 23
    buying, 39-40
    classification, 134-145
    collecting, 15-40
    first editions 18-21
    guides, 52-53, 55
    indexing, 145-152
    length, 28-29
    preserving jazz, 15-17
    sound quality, 18-19
    specialisation in collecting 22-39
    takes, 26
    vintage, 23-26
    *see also* Recording companies, Re-
        cording names
Reference books, 58-61
Reisner, R G 57
Reissues: records, 18-20, 39-40
*Reluctant art, The* 35, 66
Research, 48
Rhythm clubs, 45
*Rhythm on record*, 48
Rhythmakers, 26
Rigby, Douglas & Elizabeth, 9, 10,
    12, 13, 22
Riverside (records), 138
Robertson, Alec, 15
Rockmore, Noel, 59
Rollini, Adrian, 138, 139
Rose, Al, 32, 58, 59
Rosenkrantz, Timme, 59
Rushing, Jimmy, 33
Russell, Luis, 32
Russell, William, 17, 138

Rust, Brian, 49, 50, 51, 52, 135-139
    passim, 149
Rutgers University, 46

San Jacinto (records), 32
Sargeant, Winthrop, 65
' Satchmo and me ', 63
Schleman, Hilton, 48
Schuller, Gunther, 31, 65, 66, 137
Scott, Cecil, 139
*Second line, The*, 32
Secondary indexes, 150-151
' Sense of the past, The ', 12
Sentimentality, 33, 35-37, 67
Series, Completing a, 9, 10, 13, 22,
    38
Seventy-eight rpm records
    collecting, 23-28
    effect on jazz performances, 28
    reissues, 18-20, 39-40
    sound quality, 18
*Shadow and act*, 62
Shapiro, Nat, 63, 66
Shaw, Artie, 66
' Sheik of Araby ', 37
*Shining trumpets*, 65, 67
Simeon, Omer, 137, 139
Simon, George, 58
Singing, 35
Size of records, 130
Smith, Bessie, 30
Smith, Buster, 31
Smith, Charles Edward, 27, 52, 64,
    148
Smith, Edward Lucie, 17
Smith, Jabbo, 137
Smith, Stephen, 17, 27
Smith, Willie ' The Lion ', 63
Snowden, Elmer, 139
*So this is jazz*, 56
Social analysis, 64, 69
Solo identification, 50, 149
Souchon, Edmond, 32, 58, 59
' Soul ' music, 45
Sound quality in records, 18-19
South-west jazz, 137, 139
Spanier, Muggsy, 139
Specialisation in collecting, 22-39
Spellman, A B, 64
Spirituals, 30
*Sportin' house*, 67
Spottswood, Richard, 17
Stearns, Marshall, 46, 64

Stereo simulation, 18
Stock, Dennis, 59
Stone, Jessie, 137
*Story of jazz, The,* 64
*Story of the Original Dixieland Jazz
    Band,* 67
Storyville, 46
*Storyville,* 26, 51, 63
Styles of jazz
    arrangement of records, 134-141
    classification, 51, 77, 78
    specialization in collecting, 30-38
Surveys of jazz, 62, 68
Swaggie (records), 25, 26
' Swing goes Dixie ', 139
*Swing photo album,* 59
*Swing that music,* 66
Syncopation, 45

Takes, 26
*Taste and technique in book collect-
    ing,* 11-12
Taste in jazz, 24-25
*Teach yourself jazz,* 62, 67
Teagarden, Jack, 37, 50, 138
Terkel, Studs, 67
Territory bands, 137
Tertiary indexes, 152
Themes used in jazz, 33, 38-39, 151
Therapeutic value of collecting, 14
*These jazzmen of our time,* 66
*They all played ragtime,* 64
Third stream jazz, 38, 140
Thomas, Joe (trumpet), 18
Thomas, Kid, 26
' To his inconstant mistress ', 35
Traditional jazz, 136-139
*Treat it gentle,* 66
' Trouble in mind ', 38
*Trouble with Cinderella, The,* 66
Trumbauer, Frank, 138, 139

Tulane University, 46
Tunes used in jazz, 33, 38-39, 151

Ulanov, Barry, 59
*Urban blues, The,* 34
Utopian philosophy, 36

*VJM* (magazine), 26, 63
VJM (records), 25
Values of collecting, 11-14
' Variorum ' editions, 26
Venuti, Joe, 138, 139
Vintage collecting, 23-26
*Vintage jazz mart,* 26, 63
Vintage series (RCA), 18-19

Waller, Fats, 33, 137
Wareing, C H, 67
Waters, Howard, 50
Watters, Lu, 139
Wells, Dickie, 28
*Where's the meoldy?,* 62, 64
White styles, 137-138, 139
Whitehorn, Katherine, 10
Wilde, Oscar, 24, 33
Williams, Clarence, 137
Williams, Gene, 17
Williams, Martin, 28, 62, 64
Williams, Mary Lou, 26
Wilson, Colin, 15, 17, 44
Wilson, John S, 19, 52
Witherspoon, Jimmy, 30
Wolverines, 138
Work songs, 30
Wyler, Michael, 16, 47
Wynn, Albert, 137

Yearbooks, 62
Yeats, W B, 36
' You always hurt the one you love ',
    33-34